YOUR HEART

QUESTIONS YOU HAVE...ANSWERS YOU NEED

A PEOPLE'S MEDICAL SOCIETY BOOK

YOUR HEART

QUESTIONS YOU HAVE...ANSWERS YOU NEED

by ED WEINER
and the Staff of the
People's Medical Society

WINGS BOOKS
New York • Avenel, New Jersey

The People's Medical Society is a nonprofit consumer health organization dedicated to the principles of better, more responsive, and less expensive medical care. Organized in 1983, the People's Medical Society puts previously unavailable medical information into the hands of consumers, so that they can make informed decisions about their own health care. Knowing that consumers, as individuals or in groups, can make a difference, the society is involved in the debate over the future of the medical care system.

Membership in the People's Medical Society is $20 a year and includes a subscription to the *People's Medical Society Newsletter*. For information, write to the People's Medical Society, 462 Walnut Street, Allentown, PA 18102, or call (215) 770-1670.

This 1993 edition is published by Wings Books, distributed by Outlet Book Company, Inc., a Random House Company, 40 Engelhard Avenue, Avenel, New Jersey 07001, by arrangement with the People's Medical Society, Inc.

Random House
New York • Toronto • London • Sydney • Auckland

Printed and bound in the United States of America

Library of Congress Cataloging-in-Publication Data

Weiner, Ed.
    Your heart : questions you have—answers you need / by
Ed Weiner and the staff of the People's Medical Society.
        p.   cm.
    Originally published: Allentown, PA : People's Medical Society, c 1985.
    Includes bibliographical references.
    ISBN 0-517-08925-4
    1. Heart—Diseases—Popular works. I. People's Medical Society (U.S.) II. Title.
RC681.W39 1992
616.1'2—dc20   93-4623
                                                     CIP

8 7 6 5 4 3 2 1

CONTENTS

Acknowledgments vi

Introduction vii

Chapter 1 The Inside Story   3

Chapter 2 When Bad Things Happen to Good Hearts 18

Chapter 3 Bypass and the Alternatives 88

Chapter 4 Prevention 127

Chapter 5 Other Questions about the Heart and Its Diseases 156

Informational and Mutual Aid Groups 164

Glossary 165

Suggested Reading 174

Index 176

ACKNOWLEDGMENTS

This book has been a collaborative effort; therefore, special thanks are in order to:

Ed Weiner, who did the initial research and wrote the original manuscript.

Karla Morales, for subsequent research, writing, and editing.

Mike Donio and Krishni Patrick, for additional research and editorial input.

Linda Swank and Julie Wendt, who assisted by typing the information into our word processors.

Karen Kemmerer, who handled all the production aspects of the book.

Sharon Seng, for text design, and Tracy Baldwin, who provided the cover design.

We are also deeply indebted to the tens of thousands of consumer members of the People's Medical Society who continue to inform us of their interests and needs. It is because of them that books such as this are made possible.

INTRODUCTION

As the old song says, "You gotta have heart." You need it for life, loving, and compassion. And although we use our heart every minute of every day, most of us know very little about how it works, how it's fed, how it can stay in good shape for a long time, and what can be done if problems arise.

In *Your Heart: Questions You Have ... Answers You Need,* we provide you with all the important information you need to keep your "ticker" ticking in the most efficient way possible. And we do it in language you can understand.

Americans have more heart disease than any other major illness. It is America's number one killer. Considering such sober statistics, it is essential that you know everything possible about your heart.

As America's largest consumer health advocacy organization, the nonprofit People's Medical Society is dedicated to getting helpful and healthful information to the consumer. It is our philosophy that an informed consumer is an empowered one—a person capable of making the best health care decisions in partnership with his or her health provider.

Utilizing a question-and-answer format, *Your Heart: Questions You Have . . . Answers You Need* is a compilation of the most often asked questions and the latest research from the medical literature about matters related to the heart.

So while "you gotta have heart," you also "gotta have" information. This book is your source for the most important heart-helping facts.

Charles B. Inlander
President
People's Medical Society

YOUR HEART

QUESTIONS YOU HAVE...ANSWERS YOU NEED

*Terms printed in boldface can be found in the glossary, beginning on page 165. Only the first mention of the word in the text will be boldfaced.

1 THE INSIDE STORY

Q: Okay, let's get down to basics:
What is the heart?

A: When you pledge allegiance to the flag, you place
your right hand over your left breast, presumably
to be more in touch with your heart. No one can
challenge you on the depth of your patriotism,
but not so on the breadth of your anatomical
knowledge. Your heart isn't under your left
breast—it's a few inches over, nearly smack dab
in the middle of your chest in an area called the
mediastinum. (You can feel the beat of your
heart on the left side because the heart seems to
be tilted a bit to the left and the farthest left
part, the apex, is where the beat is perceived to
be loudest.)

The standard description of the average heart is that it is about the size of your fist, weighs less than a pound, is somewhat pear-shaped, is pinkish-gray in color, and doesn't look a thing like the drawings we make of it when we're kids. It is a muscle (**myocardium**), it's hollow, it's divided into a left and right side, each with two chambers (**atrium** and **ventricle**), it's attached to a complex freeway of arteries (complete with cloverleafs), it's the pump at the center of your circulatory system, and it's usually good to you so long as you're good to it. When the two of you have a falling out, it can be the end of a beautiful friendship—and your life.

Your heart is a well-protected piece of machinery. Though fragile in its own right, your heart sits like an oyster within a sac called the **pericardium** inside a hard shell made up of the **sternum**, or breastbone, to the front of it, the rib cage and lungs around it, the diaphragm under it, and the backbone behind it. It's a masterful design for the protection of an important package, one that M.I.T. engineers would be proud to have designed.

Q: What, exactly, does the heart do?

A: Some people call their heart "the ol' ticker," but there's really no ticking involved. Rather, the heart could more accurately be called "the ol' lub-dub-and-whoosh." To get a better view of and feel for the work your heart does, let's pretend we can shrink down to the size of a drop of your blood, and then take the journey it makes through your body. Grab your scuba gear and flashlight—next stop, the heart.

Let's start our body surfing in the heart itself; more specifically, the **left ventricle**, where the blood—tingling with oxygen and ready to travel —is propelled by a forceful contraction into the body's primary **artery**, the **aorta**. The force of the blood in the aorta, when measured, is what we've come to know as blood pressure. Coursing along the arterial system, you and countless other blood cells (and nutrients) are transported through progressively tinier and tinier blood vessels and capillaries to the body's tissues. You deliver your parcel of oxygen to the eagerly awaiting tissues, which need it to stay alive. And then, after you've collected your tip (waste products and carbon dioxide—some tip), you turn around, a little blue and winded, and follow the flow through the body's network of veins, arriving finally at the **superior** and **inferior vena cava**, and back to the heart.

In the heart, the oxygen-and-nutrient-deficient blood collects in the **right atrium**. It's then pumped out through the right ventricle into the **pulmonary artery** and off to the lungs, where the blood gladly gives up the carbon dioxide and waste (which you breathe out) and sucks up its fill of oxygen (which you breathe in). The blood flows from the lungs to the **left atrium**, where it collects, ready to move into the left ventricle, to be pumped out through the aorta to the rest of the body. And this is where we came in.

Over and over, again and again, this cyclical process—the blood moving from the upper reservoir atrium chambers to the lower pumping ventricle chambers, and out and back through 60,000 miles of veins, arteries, and capillaries—

goes on day in and day out, your heart thumping
to the rhythm of an average of 72 beats (an
average volume of six quarts of blood) every
minute that you are alive.

Q: So is it all that oxygen-rich blood pumping through it that keeps the heart healthy?

A: As a matter of fact, it isn't—at least not directly.
Despite the huge volume of blood flowing
through the heart each day (some 8,000 quarts
worth), none of it aids the heart muscle in
getting the oxygen and sustenance it needs. Like
other parts of the body, the heart receives its
"diet" via a system of arteries. These are called
the **coronary arteries**—so called because to
some anatomist's eyes, these arteries seemed to
form a thorny crown around the heart. There
are four such arteries—the right and left main,
the circumflex, and the anterior descending. As
with the rest of the body's arterial system, the
heart's blood supply derives from arteries that
come off the aorta, and split into capillaries that
feed the muscle. Then a system of veins returns
the deoxygenated blood to the right atrium.

Coronary heart disease, then, is a severe
health problem affecting not so much the
heart's muscle directly as the flow of the blood
through this "crown" surrounding and feeding
the heart.

Q: **What are heart valves? Where are they in the heart, and what do they do?**

A: The valves are extremely thin, powerful, and efficient "flood gates" made of endocardial tissue (**endocardium** is also the substance that lines the walls of the atria and ventricles). The valves, when closed, act as barriers to keep blood in areas where it should be (and from flowing back instead of forward), and then, upon opening, allow the blood to move on.

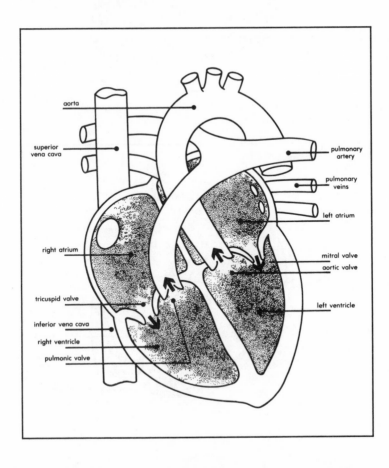

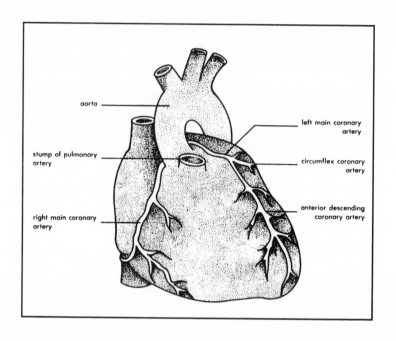

aorta

stump of pulmonary artery

right main coronary artery

left main coronary artery

circumflex coronary artery

anterior descending coronary artery

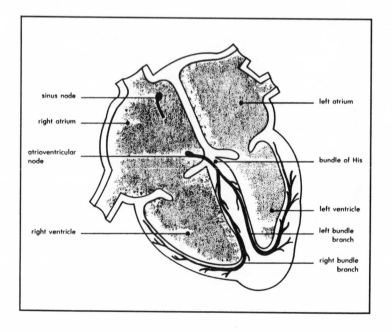

sinus node

right atrium

atrioventricular node

right ventricle

left atrium

bundle of His

left ventricle

left bundle branch

right bundle branch

There are four valves, and in the course of the blood's journey through the heart, it meets these valves somewhat in this order: As the deoxygenated blood accumulates in the reservoir of the right atrium, it is kept there by the **tricuspid valve**. When the tricuspid opens up, the blood flows into the right ventricle, and then is pumped through the **pulmonic valve** into the lungs. The now-oxygenated blood arrives in the left atrium and is kept within that chamber by the closed **mitral valve**; when the mitral opens, the blood flows into the left ventricle and is pumped through the open **aortic valve** into the aorta and off to the rest of the body. The actual rhythm has the mitral and tricuspid valves opening then closing in unison. This causes the "lub" sound of the heartbeat. Then the pulmonic and aortic valves, upon the heart's contraction, open in unison to allow the blood to flow. This causes the "dub" sound of the heartbeat.

Q: Speaking of that heart rhythm: What makes the heart contract and beat in the first place?

A: It has to do with the heart's conduction system. If that term—conduction—sounds like something out of electrical engineering, that's just about right. In the wall of the right atrium of your heart, so small that only a powerful microscope can pick it out, is something called the **sinus**, or **sinoatrial** (S-A), **node**. In simple terms, it is your heart's natural pacemaker.

What happens is that an electrical impulse from the S-A node is conducted through the atria, down to the **atrioventricular** (AV) **node** and, via right and left bundle branches, to the ventricles which, upon receiving the impulses, contract. This whole process takes less than a second. That contracting is what you call your heartbeat.

So the heart, unlike other muscles in the body, doesn't need to be stimulated by electrical nerve impulses outside itself—it can do it all, with consistency and rhythmicity. A human heart, even after being disconnected from all other nerves in the body, will continue to beat 70 to 80 times a minute. The conduction system even has a self-adjusting feature to alter the force of the contraction if the need should arise.

A word or two about the nature of the beat. There are two components to it: The **diastole** is that portion of the heartbeat when the heart is at rest—that is, when blood from the atrium is pouring into the ventricle, just before the ventricular contraction; the **systole** is the contraction. The two numbers in blood pressure readings correspond to these heartbeat phases, the systolic (or higher number) being a measurement of the blood's pressure against artery walls when the heart is at work, and the diastolic being the measurement of blood pressure during the heart's relaxation period. In a normal blood pressure reading of 120/80— or "120 over 80"—the systolic pressure is indicated by the 120, the diastolic by the 80.

Q: How do medical and health professionals know if your heart is healthy—or diseased?

A: They find out, mostly, through techniques and tools we're all relatively familiar with.

Most well-known is the **stethoscope**. Invented in the last century by a French physician, the misnamed stethoscope (the word comes from Greek roots meaning "a device for viewing the chest," which it is not, of course; it listens to the goings-on within the chest) coldly presses against our bodies from cradle to grave, sending sounds up two flexible rubber tubes to diagnostically discerning ears and brains. An experienced and knowledgeable practitioner can listen to the sounds emanating from your chest—which is a very noisy place indeed, what with all the body's mechanical doings and breathing and so on—and know which are normal and belong there, and which are out of the ordinary (murmurs, crackling and rubbing noises), might be signs of trouble, and require further investigation.

During that investigation, a **sphygmo-manometer** may be among the first devices a medical or health practitioner will turn to. A sphygmomanometer (pronounced sfig-mo-muh-NOM-itur) is the official name for what most people call a blood pressure cuff. A blood pressure reading—whether high, low, or right where it's supposed to be—will add possibly important information to the diagnostic picture your physician or nonphysician practitioner is developing.

Q: How about electrocardiograms? What do they show?

A: The **electrocardiogram** (EKG or ECG, for short) is an amplifying instrument used by physicians either on a specific mission to uncover evidence of suspected heart disease or as a routine informational step in a regularly scheduled physical examination. Among the things an EKG can show well are irregular heartbeat rhythms and signs of heart muscle damage caused by a blocked coronary artery.

An electrocardiograph machine "hears" the heart's electrical current and amplifies it about 3,000 times its normal strength. The way it does that is through a system of five to 10 electrical leads—metal plates smeared with a wet paste that aids conductivity—placed on a patient's body at locations that are key to picking up the heart's electrical impulses: the arms, the legs, and the chest. These impulses in the heart are detected by the electrodes and sent on to the EKG machine, where they move a pen in readable patterns along a continuous strip of graph paper.

Most of us have seen these long, thin, black-and-white strips of paper with the heart action scrawled along them in the form of jagged hills and valleys. Here is a typical EKG pattern of waves and spikes, and the alphabetical designations given to each segment:

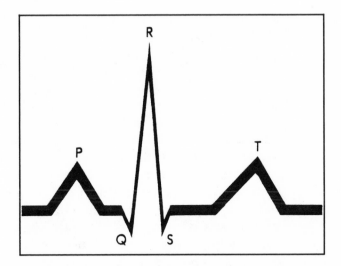

The P wave shows the electrical action within the heart as both atria contract. The Q, R, and S waves (called the QRS complex) illustrate what is going on in the ventricles. The T wave shows the ventricles recovering from one contraction and preparing for the next.

Qualified practitioners know the normal EKG patterns, and can add to their diagnosis by gauging whether what they've just recorded falls within normal ranges or, if it doesn't, what the abnormal waves and spikes suggest.

Q: How accurate is an EKG reading?

A: Pretty accurate—within limits. For one thing, a single, solitary EKG reading in a doctor's office might not show up anything wrong when there *is* indeed something wrong, because the reading happened to be taken over a period of time when that problem wasn't apparent and thus couldn't be picked up by the machinery. Then, too, a person's heart difficulties may show up only after exertion, so a reading taken while the patient is at rest might not be worth the time and money spent on the test; that's why doctors often put patients on the treadmill or up-and-down the staircase of a **stress test**, and take EKG readings before, during, and after the exercise.

As a means of recording a patient's electro-cardiogram throughout daily activities, throughout 24 hours, ambulatory electrocardiographic monitoring (AEM) devices were introduced more than 20 years ago. Since then, these devices have been used for a variety of clinical purposes, including: evaluating irregular heartbeats, called **arrhythmias**; evaluating symptoms related to arrhythmias; estimating the prognosis of heart disease; and guiding the use of antiarrhythmic drugs. You should be aware, however, that in 1990 the American College of Physicians recommended more selective and less routine use of AEM for screening or diagnosis of coronary artery disease in patients who do not display any symptoms; for prognosis after a heart attack in patients with no symptoms; and for detection of arrhythmias in people with heart disease who have no symptoms. (In this latter case, said the group, a stress EKG is a more effective alternative.)

In short, EKGs are not foolproof, they are not good predictors of soon-to-be heart disease, and they aren't immensely valuable in detecting a number of cardiovascular ills. The EKG is a good diagnostic tool—not the last word, not the end-all and be-all—and best used in concert with other examinations and tests that will help to confirm each other and the doctor's hunch.

Q: What are some of those other tests?

A: As the doctor grows more and more certain that a heart disorder—or even a particular heart disorder—is what's plaguing you, the tests become more sophisticated and complex, tend to give more information to the examining physician or technician, move into the area of invasive techniques, and carry with them slightly greater risks than EKG or stethoscope examination.

For example, your doctor might want you to have a chest X ray taken to look at heart structures or lung and blood vessel complications, or even might want to inject you with a radioactive dye, or contrast material, which allows the doctor to observe and monitor the function (or malfunction) of the heart's structures. (This latter procedure is called **angiography**.)

Echocardiography is another diagnostic technique a person with suspected heart disease might run into. In this, ultrasonic waves are aimed at and projected through the chest. These sound waves then strike the heart and its various internal structures and are bounced back. Graphic pictures, or echocardiograms, are made of these ultrasonic echoes, in much the same way that the Navy gets pictures of the ocean floor by sending sounds into the depths and obtaining a depiction of the bottom's topography based on the deflected waves. Echocardiography is a painless procedure that helps the doctor or technician "see" problems involving the heart's valves. It is far less tricky and risky than **cardiac catheterization**, although catheterization may be the only valuable technique to uncover information in certain circumstances.

Q: What is that—cardiac catheterization?

A: It's a process wherein a thin, flexible tube is inserted in a locally anesthetized patient, and then pushed along through a blood vessel (usually in the groin or arm areas) and on into the heart. To study the right side of the heart, the catheter is snaked through a vein; for the left side, an artery is used. The passage of the catheter tube is observed by doctors by using **fluoroscopy**, a specialized X-ray procedure.

When the coronary arteries are being examined, the process is referred to as **coronary arteriography**, while **angiocardiography** is the name for the test when the atria or ventricles are the targets of the probe.

Q: What is cardiac catheterization good at finding?

A: It is probably the best way yet developed for a physician to decide if heart surgery is in your immediate future. The cardiac catheterization process can tell the doctor if the oxygen content of your blood is abnormal, if your cardiac output is low, if there are structural heart defects or valve problems, or how extensive coronary artery disease is and how best to surgically attack the trouble—if surgery is the answer. The procedure has been called the gold standard for its ability to present detailed images of the heart's blood vessels.

Cardiac catheterization is not an overly risky procedure, but any time an invasive technique is used, especially one that enters the heart, there is always danger. Cardiac catheterization, though useful and relatively painless, should be performed only when absolutely necessary, and should not be taken lightly by either doctor or patient.

A growing number of doctors are criticizing the overuse of cardiac catheterization, claiming it is too dangerous (major complications and deaths have been reported) in some cases, is too freely ordered, costs too much, and is not error-free. As more than one expert in the field has cautioned: "It's a big money-maker in cardiology and, as such, there is tremendous incentive to do more and more of them." Discuss these issues and alternative procedures with your physician.

2 WHEN BAD THINGS HAPPEN TO GOOD HEARTS

Q: What is heart disease? What causes it?

A: Not an easy question to answer. That's because there is no single entity you can point to and call "heart disease." There are bushel baskets full of cardiac and circulatory problems ranging from the metabolic to the genetic to the physiologic. There is no single cause. There are lots of causes for lots of varying conditions. And sometimes there are lots of causes for just one condition, each of these different causes adding to the total picture and ultimate heart problem—and an annual medical bill for heart disease in this country that is estimated at around $101.3 billion, or 2 percent of the gross national product, or GNP. "Multifactorial" is what the medical professionals call these heart disease conditions.

In fact, if you skim through the medical literature of just the past few years, you'll find researchers ranging far and wide to find *the* cause, *the* most important element contributing to the epidemic of heart disease in America and other countries of the westernized world. Some scientists think heart disease is caused by things we do, others by things we are. Still others think one or various heart diseases are caused by things we are victim to.

Q: **What are some of these studies saying and showing?**

A: A lot of them point again and again to the best known, and what are considered the major, risk factors for those heart diseases that appear to be acquired and avoidable: cholesterol, smoking, drinking, lack of exercise, stress, obesity, high blood pressure—all of which we'll discuss in some length later on.

Beyond these, new reports seem to come out with great frequency and make splashy newspaper headlines. Some of these scientific reports underline the obvious, while others break new ground. Others border on the downright exotic (or as exotic as dry medical literature gets). And they create more questions than they answer.

For example:

• Poverty and heart disease are related, according to an American Heart Association study. Conducted in Los Angeles County, the study found that heart disease death rates increased as median family income declined.

Thus, poor white men died of heart disease more than better-off white men (a finding that reverses statistics of more than 20 years ago), poor black men died of heart disease more than better-off black men, and the same relationship holds for women. A greater percentage of black men than white men are poor; that may be why black men have a higher overall heart disease death rate.

What's the reason for the poverty/heart disease connection? According to an epidemiologist at the National Heart, Blood and Lung Institute, "The impression is that it's less well-to-do people who have maintained the bad habits while the well-off have either gotten medical care for their high blood pressure, modified their diet, or are more fitness conscious." It's also because poor people have inadequate access to health care and this, as much as life-style, could explain the higher death rate.

• Sickle cell anemia may cause heart attacks, say researchers at the University of Southern California Medical Center, and it does so without any coronary **atherosclerosis** (fatty deposits on coronary artery walls—"hardening of the arteries"). The scientists believe that in some black people (that portion of the population that has the condition almost exclusively) the sickle- or crescent-shaped blood cells may keep the heart muscle from receiving adequate oxygen supplies, leading to oxygen starvation, and ultimately **myocardial infarction** (known commonly as a heart attack, or by the initials MI).

• Estradiol (or estrogen), a female sex hormone, has been found to be present in higher levels in men who get heart attacks than in men who don't. What this could mean, say researchers from Columbia University, the National Institutes of Health, and the Framingham Heart Study, is that heart disease may be primarily a hormonal disorder. Why the high levels of a female hormone show up in some men, how it happens, and what to do about it are puzzling at the moment.

• A number of studies indicate that noise—industrial, community, and other stress-causing sounds—may lead to high blood pressure and heart problems. People who live near airports or under flight paths, according to some research, tend to have blood pressure abnormalities, higher pulse rates, and a number of other cardiovascular changes. And, worst of all, children appear to be most affected by this dangerous noise pollution.

• Higher insulin production in women than men may be the reason women generally have lower heart disease mortality and better blood-fat levels. It's not known why, exactly. It might have something to do with the way insulin acts as a hypotensive **vasodilator**—that is, as a mechanism for opening wider the blood vessels, allowing blood to flow through easier and thus reducing the force of the blood pressure. It's also been shown that diabetes tends to equalize the level of heart disease among men and women.

• Perhaps as much as 10 percent of the hundreds of thousands of sudden cardiac deaths every year in the United States may be the result of allergic reactions. Researchers have found histamine—a chemical produced in the body, especially the nasal passages and lungs, when the body comes in contact with something it is sensitive to—in human heart muscle, and this release of histamine caused the heartbeat rate to increase twofold. What the scientists are saying, in other words, is that while an allergen may affect your nose in a way that causes you to sneeze, your heart during an allergic reaction may "sneeze" in the form of sudden cardiac arrest.

• There seems to be a positive association between retirement among men and subsequent death from coronary heart disease, according to a study by doctors at the Harvard Medical School and Brigham Hospital. According to the researchers, who studied men (average age: 58) in Florida's Dade and Broward counties, the risk of heart disease among men who were retired was 80 percent higher than among those who weren't retired. Said one of the doctors involved in the study: "It is possible that we may have stumbled across a new risk factor, because many of those who die of heart attacks have none of the established risk factors, and that's why we are searching for possible psychosocial stress factors, such as retirement."

• According to a report by Boston scientists at the 1991 meeting of the American Heart Association, men whose height is 5 feet, 7 inches and under appear to be up to 70 percent more likely to have a heart attack than those who stand 6 feet, 1 inch and above. The results are similar to those from a previous study that found a higher risk of heart attacks in shorter women than in taller ones. The speculation is that smaller people have smaller coronary vessels that are more vulnerable to blockage. You might say that's the long and short of current research on heart attacks.

These are just a few. There are many others. As to which one is the real thing, *the* source of heart problems, "it"—well, it might be one of them, or a combination of a few working together. Or all. Or none. What makes people's coronary arteries clog and hearts go into spasm may be something complex or something simple that is not yet even being considered as a cardiac culprit.

While in many instances the cause of heart problems is not clear, the whats and hows of the problem are clear or clearer. When arrhythmia is the trouble, or chest pain, or heart murmur, medical experts know what is involved and what's gone wrong. In the rest of this section, we'll define and explore these illnesses, conditions, and defects.

CONGESTIVE HEART FAILURE

Q: What is **congestive heart failure?**

A: In general, what it means is that your heart is having pump problems and isn't able to keep up adequate blood circulation and oxygen transmission to the rest of the body. More specifically, it has to do with myocardial failure, especially defects of the valves, and affects the right or left ventricle. Water and sodium are inadequately eliminated, remain in the body, and can cause fluid overload leading in many cases to death by total heart failure.

Q: How does it happen?

A: There are a number of bodily failures and abnormalities, usually involving the ventricles, that cause congestive heart failure: The ventricles may not fill up with enough blood when the heart is in its diastolic, or resting, phase; they may fill up with too much blood during the systolic, or action, phase (sometimes due to high blood pressure); they may just not have enough strength to contract properly. What causes the initial ventricular problems usually falls into one of two categories: (1) either there is a mechanical obstruction or blockage of some sort, as with **aortic stenosis** (an obstruction to the flow of blood from the left ventricle to the aorta), or (2) numerous diseases, including coronary artery disease and hypertension.

Q: What are the symptoms?

A: In general, people with congestive heart failure have a tough time breathing, and as the condition worsens—as the heart pumps less and less well or effectively—frightening breathlessness, along with coughing, are commonplace. At first, physical exertion brings on attacks of wheezing and shortness of breath, but later, as the situation deteriorates, these attacks can occur even when the person is relaxing or sleeping. Lying down makes matters worse, because blood from the legs moves up to the already congested and bloated lungs. Fluid retention—in the lungs (known as **pulmonary edema**) and sometimes in the lower extremities—is another aspect of worsening congestive heart failure.

Angina pectoris—a severe, suffocating chest pain caused by an insufficient amount of blood being supplied to the heart muscle—is a symptom of left-sided congestive heart failure, and it often occurs at night. Liver pain, caused by excess fluid retention, is a symptom of right-sided congestive heart failure. And diminished urination may indicate either right- or left-sided failure.

Q: What can be done about it?

A: First of all, your body takes all this slushiness and gasping as a personal affront and tries to act in self-defense. The body revs up a few "compensatory mechanisms," as they are referred to in medical terminology, to get things back to normal. And they work . . . for a time, but they usually end up causing even more woes in the long run.

Q: What are these "compensatory mechanisms"?

A: For one, since the heart may be having weak contractions, the body decides to try to beef up the heart by building up its muscle mass (a situation known as **hypertrophy**). The idea is that more muscle means more oomph behind each heartbeat. Trouble is, the new muscle creates a need for additional oxygen, just to feed itself. And this at a time when the heart isn't doing a good job of getting oxygen out to body parts that need it desperately.

Another form of compensating takes place when the ventricles themselves expand in size so that they can hold more blood (a situation called **dilatation**). A good idea—except that the increased volume of blood being pumped leads to too much blood being poured into the blood vessels and too much fluid retention all over the body.

Also, the sympathetic nervous system picks up the tempo of the heart's beat, trying to get that blood moving out to all parts of the body. Unfortunately, this can lead to **tachycardia** (dangerous, abnormally fast heartbeat) and arrhythmia (irregular heartbeat), among other conditions.

Then, too, there are what are called peripheral mechanisms, attempts by systems not located within the heart to get things back to normal. Among these is the narrowing of arteries and veins; the body urges this to happen for a simple reason: If the amount of blood being ejected from the heart is low, a narrower pathway will keep the blood pressure up.

Q: So what if I have congestive heart failure? What kind of treatment is there for me?

A: The normal therapeutic path often starts in the hospital, where the medical people try to stabilize your deteriorating condition. By treating and correcting certain clinical conditions—certain arrhythmias can be eliminated by implanting a pacemaker, for example—some congestive heart failure may simply be cleared up. The hospital setting is supposed to provide you with needed rest—its success in this regard is questionable, at best. Techniques and technology are applied to help keep the lungs clear, the circulation moving properly, and the rest of your bodily functions working at satisfactory levels. Lots of blood will be taken for tests to check various indicators and levels, especially those having to do with possible anemia and thyroid problems.

You'll be put on a very low sodium diet, to help reduce the retention of fluid and to keep blood pressure down. Some sort of exercise plan may be prescribed to build up heart and overall body strengths (although rest is seen by many doctors as the better therapy, and that even a brief rest period during the day, at home or even at work, can do wonders for the recovering congestive heart failure sufferer).

Surgery to correct valve troubles might also be necessary.

Q: And drugs?

A: Yes, and drugs. **Digitalis** (often in the forms called digoxin or digitoxin) is the drug most often prescribed for this condition. In fact, it's one of the most often prescribed drugs in the U.S. This drug, made from the dried leaf of *Digitalis purpurea* (purple foxglove), works to strengthen the heartbeat and slow it down, and reduces the size of the enlarged heart so typical of congestive heart failure. Digitalis makes the affected heart a more efficient pump.

In addition, vasodilators are given to the congestive heart failure sufferer to allow blood to flow more freely from the heart through the body, and **diuretics** are taken to activate the speedier elimination of excess fluids from the body. These two types of medication are also commonly used to help reduce high blood pressure. Common and familiar vasodilators are nitroglycerin, minoxidil, hydralazine (Apresoline), nitroprusside, prazosin (Minipress), captopril (Capoten), and nifedipine, among others. Diuretic brand names that are widely known are Diuril, Hydrodiuril, Lasix, and Bumex.

You have to really be careful when using any drug; these are no exception, and digitalis particularly so—especially if dosing yourself at home—because its toxic dose is so close to its therapeutic dose. A little heavy on the digitalis, and you're back in the hospital, this time with digitalis intoxication. Among some of the signs of digitalis poisoning are diarrhea and vomiting, confusion, blurred or color-distorted vision, depression, a suddenly decreased heartbeat rate, or dangerous arrhythmias. Digitalis use may also lead to potassium deficiency—especially if the digitalis is taken by someone who is also taking a thiazide-type diuretic—so it's probably wise to take a potassium supplement, in potassium chloride form, at the same time. That's also a good idea because strong potassium levels may protect you from digitalis toxicity.

There are other digitalis-drug interactions, and so many ways digitalis use can be risky. A person prescribed digitalis should know why it is being prescribed, should be informed well by a medical or pharmacy professional about the proper doses and uses and about risks, and should be educated to recognize the early signs of digitalis intoxication and how to remedy it.

Q: **Are any pharmaceutical developments on the horizon?**

A: So glad you asked. According to scientists at a meeting of the American Heart Association in late 1991, a drug used to treat congestive heart failure has been found to prevent the onset of symptoms in the first place. Experts say the findings of this landmark study could lead doctors to prescribe the drug enalapril to hundreds of thousands of Americans (although it was also reported that the findings would apply to other drugs in the class as well). Enalapril, marketed by Merck as Vasotec, is one of a relatively new class of drugs known as angiotensin converting enzyme, or ACE, inhibitors—drugs which interfere with the body's production of angiotensin, a chemical that causes the arteries to constrict. ACE inhibitors are widely used to treat high blood pressure and advanced heart failure.

Researchers studied more than 4,000 people with mild to moderate congestive heart failure and found that those given the drug were 37 percent less likely to develop heart failure. In addition, there were fewer fatal and nonfatal heart attacks among people taking the drug. And very large reductions in costs resulted from lower hospitalization rates. While this idea is still rather new, it's worth talking over with your physician.

CONGENITAL HEART DEFECTS

Q: **What are congenital heart defects?**

A: They are, as the word **congenital** denotes, structural defects or abnormalities that occur at birth due to mess ups that take place in the fetus during its development and growth in the womb—in other words, portions of the heart or major blood vessels that grow incorrectly or incompletely.

Q: **How common are congenital defects?**

A: About 25,000 babies are born each year with heart defects, and there are at least 35 types of defects recognized.

Q: Is a congenital defect always a death sentence?

A: Definitely not. About 920,000 Americans with heart defects are alive today.

Q: Why do these congenital defects occur?

A: For any number of possible reasons, very few of which are completely understood by medical science. German measles (rubella) acquired by the mother early in pregnancy is a well-known cause of defects in some cases. Certain drugs seem to cause birth defects—pregnant women should be careful about what they put in their mouths. And that goes for alcohol, too. Down's syndrome children may have cardiac abnormalities. And environmental factors may contribute to some defects.

Q: How obvious are they? Are they noticed and taken care of right away?

A: By about the age of five, nearly all congenital defects have been discovered. More than half of those cases are noted during the baby's first year of life. Severe cases are often fatal very soon after birth. Others may be noted and followed through the teen years and adult life without any surgery or other treatment required.

Sometimes problems in people in their late years are due to complications of the surgery they had when they were young.

Q: **How do doctors know if you have a congenital defect or not?**

A: Usually by hearing a murmur, or out-of-the-ordinary sound, during an examination.

Q: **Do all murmurs indicate that congenital heart disease is present?**

A: The answer to that is no. Some murmurs are what are called "innocent" murmurs—not dangerous, not indicative of any disease, really—and they often occur naturally in young people and adolescents. A knowledgeable family physician or specialist can tell the difference between innocent murmurs and significant murmurs by identifying the differing hums, clicks, and vibrations heard and felt during an examination of the heart and chest area. X rays and EKGs are also used in detecting, confirming, or negating suspected significant murmurs. For more definite, conclusive determinations, people with possibly serious murmurs or newly discovered defects may be asked to undergo cardiac catheterization, but a careful doctor will hold these invasive procedures until after the

noninvasive echocardiography is performed—
and then only if surgery seems to be the route
that will be taken to correct the problem.
Echocardiography can tell the doctor a lot, and
may rule out the need for invasive—and more
dangerous—techniques. Ultrasound, **CAT scans**
(computer-enhanced views of slices of anatomy),
and **magnetic resonance imaging (MRI)** are
other methods used to get better pictures of
the heart.

Q: **What do all these tests and machines show to the doctor?**

A: They show a lot—everything from valve defects to
heart size, from blood flow to any abnormalities
of major blood vessels.

Q: **What are some of the more common congenital heart defects?**

A: Babies born with **tetralogy of Fallot** are often
referred to as "blue babies." The word tetralogy
indicates that the problem is fourfold, and these
are the four: **ventricular septal defect**, which
means that there is an unnatural opening
between the right ventricle and the left ventricle
(this is the most common congenital heart
defect in newborns); **pulmonary stenosis**, or
severe narrowing of the pulmonary artery; **right**

ventricular hypertrophy, defined as "increase of volume of the myocardium of the right ventricle"; and a defect in which the aorta gets blood from both the right and the left ventricles, called **dextroposition of the aorta**.

The cyanosis, or blue-ness, of those afflicted with tetralogy of Fallot is due to problems with oxygenation of the blood. Stunting of growth, clubbed fingers, and the coughing up of blood are some other symptoms of this condition.

Surgery to correct this problem (in some severe cases, however, surgery is unfortunately impossible) is often recommended while the child is still quite young. Some people may live to adulthood without surgery, and live near-normal lives—but they risk later complications including brain abscesses and infections of the heart.

Another condition that causes cyanosis is Eisenmenger's syndrome, another type of ventricular septal defect with additional complications.

In patent ductus arteriosus, the passage between the aorta and the pulmonary artery (the ductus arteriosus)—which remains open in the fetus until just before birth—fails to close up. The symptoms don't show up, usually, until the child is older, and then stunted growth and breathing difficulties become apparent.

Surgery can shut the opening, and, if performed early enough (before the child reaches the teen years), there's no reason a long, productive life can't result.

Another difficulty caused by a natural opening in the fetal heart that fails to close before birth is atrial septal defect. Symptoms may not show up until adulthood, when surgery can correct it.

The problem involved with coarctation of the aorta is that a congenital defect narrows the major vessel—it may even block it entirely. This can cause really high blood pressure, especially after exercise, because the normal, forceful thrust of blood from the heart meets tremendous resistance when it rushes into the ''knob,'' or narrowed portion, of the misshapen aorta.

HEART VALVE DISEASE

Q: What is valvular heart disease?

A: To understand that, you first have to have a pretty good idea of what the valves look like and what they do.

The valves, as we've noted before, stand like sentries all along the path the blood takes going into, through, and out of the heart. When they are healthy, the valves, when open, allow blood to move in the proper forward direction; when closed, the valves prevent the blood from streaming backwards. The valves' unique construction—separate thin leaves that flap open to form a mouth to let the flow through, then flap together and shut tight like lips— acts as a levee against any backwash (**valvular regurgitation**).

Certain diseases or conditions damage the valves. For instance, **rheumatic fever** leads to **endocarditis**. This is an inflammation of the heart's inner lining that can affect the valves.

As they heal, the valves' flaps develop scar tissue, and this prevents them from closing tightly together. Blood can then leak through the gnarled opening either backward or forward (sometimes as much as 50 percent of the ejected blood, or more in very bad cases). Doctors often hear this as a murmur. The scarring can also lead to a narrowing (or stenosis) of the valve opening. This condition worsens, and usually requires surgery to repair or replace the valve.

Another way the valve leaflets degenerate is through thickening or calcification. And there are a number of additional, nonrheumatic valve disorders: floppy valve syndrome (which is pretty much what is sounds like), syphilitic heart disease, certain tumors, and drug-induced valvular difficulties, among others.

The heart chambers need to work harder to keep up the proper pumping pressure despite the narrowings and the leaks, and this frequently leads to serious complications affecting the size of the ventricles, the thickness of the ventricle walls, and just plain overwork of the pumping mechanism.

Q: How do doctors determine for sure that what I have is heart disease?

A: The usual assortment of technological steps, which should move up the ladder from noninvasive (stethoscope, fluoroscope, echocardiography) to invasive (cardiac catheterization, angiography). Most experts agree that the most conclusive kind of information about the extent of valve damage and all the complications caused by the valve damage comes from cardiac catheterization and angiography.

Q: What kind of surgery can I expect if I have valve troubles?

A: Well, that depends on the nature of the problem and its extent.

There is a procedure called **commissurotomy**, in which valve leaflets—stuck together because of the scar tissue formed after a bout with rheumatic-fever-induced endocarditis—are separated. This procedure doesn't always have to be done as open-heart surgery—during which the heart is stopped and blood flow is detoured through a heart-lung machine—but sometimes can be done while the heart continues its work. In commissurotomy, either a special tool or simply the surgeon's finger is used to separate the scar-sealed leaves. Another operation, called **annuloplasty**, is sometimes suggested. In this, the surgeon actually reconstructs the valve tissue in a kind of plastic surgery technique.

Unfortunately, in some cases the leaves are in too bad shape, or they go back to sticking to each other again. That's when further surgery— usually valve replacement—is called for.

Q: **How safe is valve replacement surgery?**

A: Within limits, it's safe. But any operation has its risks—especially when you fiddle around with the heart—and valve surgery certainly has its share, including subsequent complications with the new valves and the danger of rejection.

Q: **What are those complications?**

A: The replacement valves placed in your heart to do the job of your diseased mitral or aortic valves are in one way or another fashioned by human hands. Some—called prosthetic valves—are entirely synthetic, made of plastics, cloth, metal, and other molded and shaped products. These last quite a while.

An alternative is an aortic valve taken from a pig, or valves made of other tissue, attached to a ring or skin graft mold.

There are possible problems and complications attached to both of these. The plastic type sometimes ''throws a clot''—that is, it creates a **thromboembolism** (blood clot) that blocks up a blood vessel. This can be really serious, and blood clots of this sort showing up in the wrong place can lead to life-threatening crises. Recipients of artificial valves are often prescribed so-called blood-thinning drugs to try to prevent this clotting problem.

Other complications include separation of the ring from where it is attached to the heart, infection, and—in tissue replacement valves—

deterioration or calcification similar to what happened to the original valves, sometimes within 10 to 15 years of implant. Frequently, valve difficulties show up in a heart that is also suffering from coronary artery disease, which brings in a whole load of its own complications, as we'll soon see. Some surgeons may want to perform coronary artery bypass surgery at the same time they put in a new valve. (A discussion of bypass surgery and alternatives can be found later in this book.)

The type of surgery for your condition, the type of valve if replacement is necessary, the need for simultaneous bypass surgery, and the risks and complications involved should all be discussed with the surgeon before a decision is made and consent given.

Q: Any other complications?

A: A few postoperative ones, especially the danger of endocarditis occurring or recurring. Infection is a tremendous threat to the re-valved heart, and thus operations like dental surgery and others should be accompanied by careful and sufficient antibiotic treatment.

Anticoagulants, which probably must be taken for life in those with prosthetic valves, can be worrisome, and especially so in women who become pregnant. The blood-thinners may cause miscarriages or birth defects. That's why women of childbearing age who need heart valve replacement might be wise to opt for the tissue-type valve implant, which may not require anticoagulant therapy.

It's also been reported that prosthetic valve implantation may be a factor in the development of gallstones.

HEARTBEAT IRREGULARITIES

Q: What are heartbeat irregularities?

A: During attacks of irregular heartbeat, the heart just seems to go crazy, speeding up or slowing down, or fluttering and contracting out of control. It can be absolutely frightening when this occurs to you suddenly, or even if it is a frequent event, because that critical organ inside you that has always been faithful and quiet and true now has a wild, electrically misfiring mind of it own. And you feel as if you can't do a thing about it.

Conditions of abnormal heartbeat and rhythm, known generally as arrhythmias, have a multitude of causes, a wide variety of ways they display themselves, and—luckily—a fairly well established set of responses for controlling or eliminating them.

Some of the things that set off arrhythmias are: a diminished amount of oxygen reaching the heart muscle (**hypoxia**), an unnaturally slow heartbeat (**bradycardia**), a blockage that causes a reduced or stopped flow of blood (**ischemia**), certain kinds of drugs, and other changes in the physical, electrical, or chemical properties of the heart.

Sometimes arrhythmias occur in people with heart disease who are taking digitalis, especially if digitalis toxicity is present or if the person is potassium-deficient (a possible side effect of having taken diuretics), magnesium-deficient, or has too much calcium in the blood.

Q: Are all arrhythmias life-threatening?

A: No. Nearly all of us have had an arrhythmic episode at one time or another. That's when, for no apparent reason, we feel an odd "flip-flop" in our heart, or it feels as if it just stopped for a second. Hearts do that every once in a while—a little dirt on the spark plugs, probably —and it usually doesn't mean much. Drugs or other therapy are probably not required, unless those strange doings persist.

Even some of the more serious arrhythmias aren't of grave concern of and by themselves, although they may be signs that a worrisome heart condition is present or that some other physical problems exist.

Q: For example?

A: Well, for example, there is **sinus bradycardia**. This is a very slow heartbeat, 60 beats per minute or less when the heart is at rest.

Sometimes this is simply a normal state of affairs for runners and marathoners, but it may also be a sign of **hypothyroidism** and **hypothermia**, to name just two. And certain prescribed drugs, especially tranquilizers, have a bradycardiac effect.

A more violent type of attack takes place during **atrial paroxysmal tachycardia**, which is pretty much the opposite of bradycardia. Here, the heart (actually, the atria) suddenly takes off at a gallop, with beats of up to 220 a minute, and just as suddenly returns to normal. The accelerated heartbeat is, curiously, not wild and out of control but absolutely regular—just super-fast. These tachycardias happen to people with perfectly normal hearts as well as to those who have congenital defects. The attacks are usually not dangerous or life-threatening, unless some sort of heart disease is also present. Normally, medical attention is not necessary— dunking your face into cold water pretty much stops the problem—but if the condition persists, drugs or electrical therapy may be necessary.

A few of the most common of the many types of arrhythmias that respond to therapy are **atrial flutter, atrial fibrillation, sick sinus-node syndrome,** and **heart block**.

Q: **Which is the most serious of the arrhythmias?**

A: Almost certainly it's **ventricular fibrillation**. In this cardiac arrhythmia, the ventricle muscle contracts wildly and out of control, the aortic valve refuses to open, and blood stops being pumped. Ventricular fibrillation often happens early in a heart attack. Ventricular fibrillation is divided into a primary phase, during which immediate therapy may save a life, and a secondary phase, which is the sign of the end. Secondary fibrillation is almost always fatal.

Q: How are arrhythmias treated?

A: In a number of ways, including medication, physical external resuscitation, and electrical stimulation. They are used in different ways for different types of arrhythmia.

Q: Could you explain how these work?

A: Sure. Let's take medications first. There are a number of drugs that can calm down the arrhythmic heart, usually by directly affecting the heart's electrical conduction system. Some of the better known and most often prescribed drugs for arrhythmia are quinidine (a relative of the antimalarial drug quinine, quinidine is used in cases of tachyarrhythmias in both the atria and ventricles), lidocaine (a local anesthetic used to control ventricular arrhythmias), propranolol (used for atrial flutter or fibrillation; also when stress causes arrhythmias, when digitalis toxicity leads to ventricular arrhythmias, and in cases of heart attack), and procainamide, among others. Each does something different in its own way, and each has a litany of side effects including gastrointestinal disorders, rashes, and occasionally more serious complications—for example, propranolol use can lead to congestive heart failure in some people.

These are potent drugs whose use and dosage sizes have to be precise.

Q: And external resuscitation?

A: The method used—keeping the heart and lungs operating during cardiac arrest by physically pressing against the heart and breathing into the lungs—is called **cardiopulmonary resuscitation**, or **CPR**. It is a widely used lifesaver that anybody can do and everybody should know. Get in touch with the local chapter of the American Heart Association or your neighborhood Y to find out about courses in CPR. Knowing it could save the life of someone you love.

Q: You mentioned electrical stimulation as a technique used against arrhythmias. What kind of electrical stimulation? How does it work?

A: The thinking goes that since the disturbances in the heart that cause arrhythmias are generally electrical in origin, then they can be set right by throwing electricity back at them. Fighting fire with fire. And that thinking works a lot of the time.

The first way electricity is used to fight arrhythmias is in the case of life-threatening ventricular fibrillations. The piece of technology involved is called, of all things, a **defibrillator**, and it's basically two metal paddles connected to a source of high-voltage electricity. When a person goes into ventricular fibrillation and the heart is going crazy, electrically speaking, these paddles—held by a qualified professional who is very well grounded and insulated—are placed either on the person's chest or, in some cases, directly on the heart itself.

Through these paddles and into the body passes a jolt so powerful that it actually throws the switch on the heart's electrical impulses and cuts off the juice, so to speak. Then the heart's natural pacemaker steps in, regains control over the heartbeat, and gets things back to normal, with help from CPR, medication, and fluids administered at the same time.

Not all defibrillating works, and when it does work the effects don't always last. People in ventricular fibrillation who are shocked back to regular heartbeat are obviously people with sick hearts, and may at any time start fibrillating again. They have to be watched very carefully.

There are side effects to defibrillation—from burnt skin caused by the voltage to cardiac arrest and even brain damage—but the benefit is certainly worth the risk.

Q: Is there any other way electrical stimulation helps people with arrhythmias?

A: There is a lot of excitement surrounding relatively new devices called automatic defibrillators, which are available in any hospital or medical center offering cardiac care. These little boxes are placed in the chest, attached to the heart of people who have had or continue to have episodes of ventricular fibrillation. The automatic implantable defibrillator actually senses fibrillation about to happen and gives off an electric charge that stops it before it gets going.

This device may become a widespread and popular lifesaving tool. Until that time, the most important electrical stimulation mechanism used to fight arrhythmias remains the artificial pacemaker.

Q: How do pacemakers work?

A: Pacemakers are tiny, lightweight mechanisms placed in the chest (although temporary pacemakers are usually not implanted) that give off an electrical charge. This charge takes over the job of the heart's own faulty natural pacemaker and keeps the heartbeat regular. The charge is generated by long-lasting batteries in the pacemaker, and is carried to the heart via a wire at the end of which is an electrode. The electrode is placed at the right ventricle during a procedure that takes about a half hour to 90 minutes (although a hospital stay could be involved). The pace of the desired beat may be adjusted at a fixed rate by the cardiologist or other medical personnel. Many pacemakers work "on demand," kicking in and taking over only when conditions require them to do so; this lets the heart's own natural pacemaker stay on the job when and as long as it can. Modern, computerized printed circuitry has allowed for reduction in the size of pacemakers (they're about the size of a silver dollar, weighing about two ounces) and a terrifically increased number of jobs the pacemaker can do. In fact, some pacemakers can be hooked up to a telephone and readings can be sent via phone lines to monitoring equipment in a doctor's office or a hospital clinic.

Two conditions that usually call for a pacemaker are: complete heart block—in which the heart's own electrical transmission reaches the atria but is not conducted to the ventricles, thus causing the atria and ventricles to beat at different rates—and sinus node difficulties.

Pacemakers are the true marvels of medical high technology, keeping people alive who just a few years ago would have been sure goners. But they, and the way they are administered, are not without drawbacks and controversy.

Q: Really? What are these drawbacks?
How serious are they?

A: As we become more and more sophisticated in the realm of technology, mechanical complications and failures are becoming rarer. Still, more often than anybody would like, there are such negative events, when pacemakers go on the fritz (and cause the same reaction in the people attached to them) because of simple mechanical flaws, sudden battery drain, and detached electrodes or broken wires. Occasionally a pacemaker goes haywire and actually creates arrhythmias. Sometimes the ventricle is accidentally punctured by the pacemaker parts, sometimes (as with any operation) infection and other problems occur.

Luckily, since the procedure is a relatively common one, there is a lot of expertise and information about implanting and repairing pacemakers, and really scary troubles are infrequent.

However, precisely because the procedure is a relatively common one—perhaps *too* common —a debate about pacemaker implants has been raging for years, and continues today.

Q: What's the debate all about?

A: It has to do with greed and kickbacks and Medicare fraud. Simply, it's all about doctors implanting too many artificial pacemakers because it's a big money-maker (a pacemaker can cost a heart patient as much as $5,000, plus hospital and physician's fees that could add up to three times that amount). There is documentation that people with ill hearts not requiring pacemakers, and people with completely healthy hearts, may have received pacemakers in the past. And such false prescribing is still going on. Federal government figures say that more than 200,000 pacemakers of the approximately one million in use today have been implanted needlessly, at a cost of $1 billion a year, plus uncountable pain and suffering.

Why have doctors put in pacemakers where none were called for? Certainly, misdiagnoses are occasionally at fault, as is incompetence. In a shockingly large number of cases, though, doctors have received kickbacks from pacemaker sales representatives and manufacturers to implant their brand of device. According to information coming out of United States Senate hearings, these kickbacks ranged from large amounts of money to free vacation trips to Europe.

Furthermore, since doctors have been able to get Medicare monies for regular monitoring of patients' pacemakers, too many of them have filed excessive or phony reports, submitting bills for patients who hadn't been monitored, or even seen. Some were even dead. But this didn't stop doctors from "monitoring" their "progress" —and asking for Medicare remuneration.

Ralph Nader's Public Citizen Health Research Group looked into pacemaker implantation in Maryland, and concluded that as many as 35 percent of these procedures were unnecessary. Pacemaker companies and medical societies claim this figure is at least 10 to 20 times too high. Yet the furor was great enough—and,

presumably, the scandal real enough—that
guidelines for appropriate use of pacemakers
were developed by the Joint American College
of Cardiology and American Heart Association
Task Force on Assessment of Cardiovascular
Procedures.

Furthermore, the Health Care Financing
Administration (the agency that oversees
Medicare) has asked the Agency for Health Care
Policy and Research to develop evaluation
standards for pacemakers. These standards are
designed to help identify likely candidates for
pacemakers and eliminate the unnecessary
implantations, which are estimated at 20 to
35 percent.

Q: **How can I be sure the pacemaker being
recommended for me is necessary?**

A: Select a highly recommended, board-certified
cardiologist who believes in discussing things
with his or her patients before going ahead with
risky and/or expensive procedures. Make an
appointment to interview this physician to make
certain he or she is the one for you.

No matter what is recommended, get a second
opinion from an independent source, not
somebody suggested by your physician; he or
she might be sending you to a friend or a
colleague who doesn't ever disagree with
what's been suggested by the first physician.
You can get names of cardiologists from a local
hospital, if it has a referral service.

Try to be admitted to a hospital that has initiated peer review of pacemaker implant procedures. Peer review means that doctors assess the procedures of other doctors to determine if the procedures are necessary, proper, and performed well and in accordance with current techniques. Studies show that hospitals with peer review committees show a decline in the number of implants and a longer survival rate among those who receive the pacemakers under the scrutiny of peer pressure.

Q: **Pacemakers and the operation that attaches them to the heart are pretty expensive. Will they get any cheaper?**

A: Don't hold your breath. Declining prices for medical items and procedures are about as common as water skiing in the Mojave Desert. Once doctors and hospitals get a good hold on a good dollar figure, that figure rarely goes down, even if the procedure is done frequently, takes less time, and the materials don't cost as much as they used to. These kinds of operations are called "winners"—when we discuss bypass surgery later on, that term will pop up again.

Medicare has attempted to put a cap on costs by instituting diagnosis-related groups (DRGs), nearly 500 conditions over which the government is imposing some monetary controls. By paying only so much for a procedure and allowing only so much time for a hospital stay, money that Medicare used to pay indiscriminately and on demand is now more frugally parceled out.

HEART MUSCLE DISEASES

Q: What can go wrong with the heart muscle itself?

A: Too much. Heart muscle disease—**cardiomyopathy**, to use the proper medical terminology—affects that part of the heart that gets behind the force of the pumping action. In cardiomyopathies—and there are numerous types raising numerous hells—the heart walls may thicken, or become rigid and inflexible, or shrink to smaller than normal size, or balloon out to a disproportionate size. Each of these abnormalities causes a serious problem, including congestive heart failure, reduced cardiac output, valvular regurgitation, and others.

Q: Why and how does the heart muscle become diseased?

A: To be perfectly honest, nobody knows what causes a substantial number of cardiomyopathies. They are mysteries, medical magnets attracting all sorts of conjecture and experimentation.

But then there are just as many or more about which a lot is known and the causative culprits have been singled out. Infections are responsible for a large number of heart muscle disorders, and some nutritional deficiencies (selenium is one) are also to blame. Illnesses and metabolic imbalances can lead to cardiomyopathies.

Degenerative diseases of the muscles, like muscular dystrophy, may affect the heart as well. High blood pressure is, of course, also among the hazards, because over years of force and overexerting the heart muscle it builds up a bulky, rigid left ventricle, and that leads to serious heart failures.

Toxic substances are prime offenders, too. And by toxic substances is meant a large number of chemicals and even pharmaceuticals that come into too close a contact with or are too massively consumed by a person. These include such different items as carbon tetrachloride and anticancer chemotherapy drugs. But the most frequently pointed-to bad guy in the cardiomyopathy toxin lineup is alcohol. Even little bits of it in mild cocktail form can throw the heart muscle for a loop.

Q: What are the symptoms of cardiomyopathy?

A: That's a tough question to answer, because each heart muscle disease is different, causes different discomforts and dangers, and is treated in a different manner. Many, if not most, lead to congestive heart failures because of the enlarged ventricle and diminished pumping power. Fainting (known as **syncope**), angina, and breathing difficulties are among other indications of possible cardiomyopathy.

As for treating these conditions, again it's a matter of the right strategies utilized to fight various and particular problems. In cardiomyopathies that lead to congestive heart failure, one accepts the cardiomyopathy and attacks the congestion by using salt reduction and high blood pressure-reducing drugs, to name just a couple of techniques. In some other types of cardiomyopathy, especially when an anatomical obstruction is the problem, surgery is usually the road taken. In some instances, unfortunately, neither medicine nor surgery can help. In these cases, where a disease has pretty much infiltrated and damaged the heart muscle irreparably, death by heart failure or heartbeat disorders is the usual end product.

PERICARDIAL DISEASE

Q: What's this one all about?

A: Well, you may remember way back in the answer to the first question we mentioned the pericardium, which is the "fluidy" sac the heart sits in. This part of the heart's family, like all the others, is prone to diseases of its own, and is an indicator of infections and/or diseases elsewhere in the body that have traveled to the region of the heart, causing many forms of **pericarditis**, or inflammation of the pericardium.

Q: What are some of the most common types of pericarditis? How are they treated?

A: In **acute pericarditis**, the infected pericardium causes chest pain when the person with the condition breathes in, fever, and a sound (heard through a stethoscope) of a dry friction in the sac. EKGs also show irregularities that are signs of acute pericarditis. It is treated by alleviating the general infection that caused it, through antibiotics and anti-inflammatory medications such as cortisone. Acute pericarditis may have other causes—wounds, tumors, etc.—that need to be treated before the pericardial infection can be eliminated. **Acute nonspecific pericarditis** is a condition in which the pericarditis is not secondary to another disease, but rather is attacked directly itself by a virus.

Unlike acute pericarditis, where the sac may be dry and fibrous (that's why there's scratchy friction), **pericardial effusion** is the name of a condition in which the pericardium becomes somewhat flooded with liquid. The liquid, or effusion, comes either from outside the pericardium or from the pericardium itself due to injury. The injury to the pericardium may come from certain drugs (minoxidil, an antihypertensive drug, is thought to be one of them); from certain cancers, and ironically, from the radiation therapy used to fight cancers; from previous heart surgery; and as a symptom of kidney failure requiring immediate dialysis. The fluid isn't always a problem in and of itself, but rather a sign of some other existing condition. However, if there is too much fluid in the pericardium, it can actually squeeze and compress the heart, getting in the way of the heart's filling up with blood; this is called **cardiac tamponade**. Pericardial effusion can be treated medically, usually to overcome the tamponade. One of several approaches may be utilized, including **pericardiocentesis** (drainage of the fluid) and surgery.

A number of the situations that are responsible for acute pericarditis and pericardial effusion—kidney failure, radiation, and tuberculosis, to name a few—may lead to another, quite serious problem called **constrictive pericarditis**. In this, the sac becomes scarred and hard and full of calcium deposits. The heart is no longer free to move about and its duties are interfered with. In essence, the heart becomes a prisoner, caught in a rigid web that used to be its soft, flexible cushion. Surgical removal of the pericardium is what's done to set things right, although this is a potentially dangerous procedure: One slip of the knife and the heart gets punctured.

Besides these pericardial problems there are others that are more rare, including tumors and congenital defects.

ANGINA AND HEART ATTACKS: ISCHEMIC HEART DISEASE

Q: What does that mean— "ischemic heart disease"?

A: Well, ischemia means that a blood vessel has become either narrower than normal or blocked up altogether, causing a deficiency or total

cutoff of blood (and thus oxygen) supply.
When this narrowing or blockage occurs in
the coronary arteries, it's known as ischemic
heart disease. When doctors refer to ischemic
heart disease, it's usually angina pectoris and
myocardial infarction that they're speaking of.

Q: **I've heard of angina attacks, and I know
many people suffer greatly from them.
What are they? What happens during an
angina attack?**

A: Especially when the coronary arteries are closed
by 50 percent or more, the stage is set for angina.
Great globs of fatty deposits called **plaque**
slathered on the artery walls because of the
progress of atherosclerosis—the most prevalent
form of "hardening of the arteries" in the U.S.
—are a major cause of narrowing, accounting
for about 90 percent of cases. Stenosis, or actual
narrowing of the vessels, is a frequent occurrence. Rheumatoid arthritis, systemic lupus
erythematosus, and other diseases may also get
in the way of normal blood flow. All these, plus
the incidence of coronary artery spasms,
contribute to conditions just ripe for angina
attacks, which are themselves not a disease but
symptoms of an underlying heart disease.

What happens is this: During physical exertion,
during stress or an emotionally charged
situation, in cold weather, or after a big meal,
the heart beats faster and requires more
oxygenated blood flow to the heart muscle to
maintain the beating. But if the channels by

which the blood and oxygen flow to the heart are narrowed, not enough nutrients get to the heart muscle tissue. It suffers oxygen deficiency, and the pain is angina pectoris.

And what a pain. It's a heavy, strangulating, suffocating experience—far more intense than anything indigestion, chest wall injuries, **pleurisy**, or spasms of the esophagus may throw your way—that seems to start under the breastbone, on the left side of the chest, and sometimes radiates out to other places: throat, neck, jaw, left shoulder and arm, and occasionally on to the right side. It is an intense, scary episode—but with rest and calm (or by placing nitroglycerin or another kind of nitrate under the tongue), angina attacks usually go away in about 15 minutes or so. If they last longer than that, a hospital trip is the wisest next step, because long-lasting angina attacks may be the prelude to heart attacks.

The statistics show that half of those with angina pectoris suffer sudden deaths, a third have heart attacks, and most victims are older men. And an estimated 300,000 new cases of angina occur each year.

Still, some doctors call angina ''God's gift to man'' because many heart problems are silent, without symptoms, and go unnoticed until they become the cause of sudden death. Angina, they say, at least announces that something's wrong.

Q:

How can the doctor tell if what I have is angina pectoris and heart disease or something else that behaves similarly?

A:

Most angina, as we said, is unmistakable, but not all. Sometimes noncardiac conditions may cause pain that mimics or comes close to feeling like angina. To determine what's what, the physician will revert to the usual set of diagnostic tools: stethoscope; electrocardiogram, which should be taken during a pain episode (to help prove it really is angina and to determine which coronary arteries are involved); stress test, on a treadmill or exercise bicycle, with EKG readings that will show coronary artery disease and indications of reasons for anginal pain; and angiography, which tells more than any other procedure, but which holds slightly more risk of injury or death from the test than the others mentioned above.

In fact, according to an international group of researchers, some patients with low to medium risk of coronary death may be undergoing angiography procedures, which are invasive and more expensive (average cost somewhere around $3,400), when a stress test would suffice and be more appropriate. (Rand Corporation—a renowned research organization—and panels of doctors estimate that 17 percent of coronary angiographies are, in their words, "unjustified," and 9 percent are "debatable.") A 1991 article in *Medical Tribune* reported the risk of heart attack or death from angiography at about one in 1,000, compared to about one in 10,000 with exercise stress testing.

Q: So how is angina treated?

A: Behaviorally, medically, and/or surgically.

A change in behavior, trying to keep calm and handling emotions better and more productively, can work toward limiting the recurrence of anginal episodes. Of course, this just delays or mitigates the symptoms; it doesn't do anything to treat the underlying physical causes of the heart pains.

In a way, that can be said for medication, too. The drugs now available for use in treating angina don't permanently clean up the narrowed areas and make things right again. Instead, they artificially alter the physiological situation and ease the heart's work. They do this by working to reduce blood pressure, widening the blood vessels in order to let blood flow through more easily, and by slowing down the heart rate to reduce the heart muscle's oxygen requirements.

Calcium channel blockers are strong pharmaceuticals used to relieve angina symptoms in those people who suffer attacks even at rest, while lying down, or sleeping, as well as at other times. Some better known and frequently prescribed calcium channel blockers are the antiarrhythmic verapimil (Calan, Isoptin), diltiazem (Cardizem), and nifedipine (Procardia). Each has its side effects—dizziness and headache, for example—with nifedipine perhaps having the most and diltiazem the least.

Use of thiazide types of blood pressure-lowering medication (diuretics) and digitalis, when congestive heart failure is a factor, are two other drug regimens to combat angina.

The classic treatment for angina, however, is nitroglycerin or other drugs in the nitrate family—Isordil and Cardilate, to name a couple. These nitrates act as vasodilators, widening the veins and arteries. They are taken in lots of different ways: Sometimes they are swallowed; occasionally they're injected intravenously. But more usually they are placed under the tongue. These days a patch containing a day's dose of nitroglycerin is placed against the body, and the nitroglycerin is dispensed transdermally—that is, it passes directly through the skin into the bloodstream. These transdermal slow-release patches are being used more and more as a way to keep angina attacks from happening, and are far more practical than under-the-tongue pops of nitrate. For one thing, there's no fumbling for nitro pills while in the throes of an attack. Further, the patches last 24 hours; a nitroglycerin pill is good for relieving angina pain, but for only about a half hour or so. Also, a nitroglycerin spray is newly available—it's sprayed under the tongue during an attack.

It is common for doctors to prescribe nitrates and calcium channel blockers at the same time because they help each other out.

Q: **And what about surgery?**

A: The surgical route is coronary artery bypass grafting—what we all know simply as bypass surgery.

We'll be getting to that, and the alternatives to bypass, right after we take a good, hard look at heart attacks.

Q: What exactly *is* a heart attack?

A: Militarily speaking, it's rather less an attack than a siege. That is, a blood clot (**thrombosis**) settles itself into a coronary artery and causes an **occlusion**, or blockage, of that artery. Blood full of oxygen destined for the heart muscle, or myocardium, is cut off before delivery. What you have is a siege leading to starvation of a portion of the heart muscle. That section of the heart muscle in turn suffers an **infarction**, a damaged or cell-dead (**necrotic**) area of tissue, usually in the left ventricle.

Q: Where do these occlusions come from?

A: They're usually the result of arteriosclerotic plaque in the coronary arteries, leading to injuries, clots, and obstruction.

(Heart attacks are also caused by other factors, like shock, overexertion, or other conditions that force the heart to require more oxygenated blood.)

The risk of heart attack death by coronary occlusion depends on how great a percentage of the blood-carrying vessel is blocked and just where the occlusion occurs.

Q: How can I tell if I'm having a heart attack?

A: You'll know. There's nothing quite like a heart attack. An angina attack is amateur hour compared to it. A powerful, crushing, breathtaking pain hits the chest and seems to flow out to the left arm, back, shoulder, and throat. The face becomes pale and is doused in a cold, clammy sweat. There is occasionally vomiting—that's why some people at first think that they're merely having a bout of bad indigestion. Many people, in pain and full of panic (which just makes things worse), pass out. Many never regain consciousness—too much heart muscle damage has been caused by an occlusion in a major artery.

For angina sufferers, a heart attack pain may initially seem like just another, although more stunning, angina episode. But when nitroglycerin has no effect, and the attack goes on beyond the usual 15 minutes or so—in fact, it may go on for hours (and many people, not believing or willing to face the idea that they are having a heart attack, wait as long as three hours or more before getting help)—it's time to get medical assistance pronto.

That's how *you* can tell if you're having a heart attack. The way doctors tell is by observing the all-too-familiar signs, through EKG readings that indicate disturbance and damage, and through blood tests that measure the change in levels of certain key enzymes.

Q: Does a person's age or gender put him or her at greater risk for a heart attack?

A: Based on the Framingham Heart Study, 5 percent of all heart attacks occur in people under age 40, and 45 percent occur in people under age 65. And in general, coronary heart disease rates are higher for males than for females. Brand-new research on the subject of gender, however, has added a twist to the gender question: In the largest study ever to compare men and women's heart attacks, researchers at the University of Rochester School of Medicine report that women who have heart attacks are 1.5 times more likely than men to die in the hospital and 1.3 times more apt to die within a year. Doctors have long considered heart disease milder in women than in men, said the study's author in a *Circulation* article, but this study shows doctors *must* "take women's cardiac symptoms very seriously and treat them as aggressively as possible."

Another recent study took a similar look at the broader issue of sex differences in the management of coronary artery disease. As reported in a July, 25, 1991, issue of *New England Journal of Medicine*, researchers concluded that despite the fact that coronary artery disease is the leading cause of death in women, "physicians pursue a less aggressive management approach to coronary disease in women than in men, despite greater cardiac disability in women."

Q: What is a "silent heart attack"?

A: It's just that—silent, undetected. About one-quarter of all heart attacks are not recognized when they occur. Many people have such "silent attacks" and never know it, although they may vaguely remember an incident where they felt inexplicably ill and full of foreboding or had a bout with unusual "indigestion." The so-called silent heart attack causes myocardial damage, but no noticeable symptoms—and sometimes no lasting problems, thereby enabling the attackees to live to long, fruitful old age never knowing that they've played host to such an event.

On the other hand, say cardiologists, these people have heart disease just as serious and potentially deadly as someone who cannot walk a flight of stairs without chest pain or someone who was hospitalized for weeks with an unmistakable heart attack. The feeling among experts is that unless these people's coronary problems are recognized and treated they could suffer a sudden and possibly fatal heart attack. Each year approximately 350,000 Americans who had no symptoms die suddenly and are found at autopsy to have had extensive coronary disease.

A silent heart attack shows up on EKG readings and during treadmill exercise stress tests, but doctors are hesitant to suggest exercise stress tests for every adult to detect those with ischemia. Why? Because costs would be high, and many **false-positive results** would lead to unnecessary follow-up tests for a lot of people.

Q: So who should be tested for silent attacks?

A: Cardiologists urge exercise stress tests for people who might be at especially high risk. These are the groups who fall into that category: (1) previously sedentary men over 35 years old and women over 50 who are about to start a vigorous exercise program; (2) men over 35 and women over 50 who have several major risk factors for heart disease—high cholesterol, high blood pressure, smoking, overweight, high stress level, or a family history of heart attack, angina, or sudden death occurring before age 60; and (3) anyone who has suffered a previous heart attack or angina, even though they may now be free of symptoms.

Q: How is a heart attack treated medically?

A: That depends on when you're talking about. Immediately at the onset of a heart attack, the victim needs to be made as comfortable and unconfined as possible: placed in a supine position, with tight collars, belts, cuffs, and shoes loosened, and cardiopulmonary resuscitation begun immediately if the heart and breathing have stopped. These are measures any of us can and should take.

The next step is medical attention. (Interestingly, studies indicate that half of all heart attack victims wait more than two hours before getting help.) In heart attack emergencies, injections of painkillers like morphine sulfate are given. Intravenous nitroglycerin may be started. Depending on whatever other physiologic conditions occur during this time—blood pressure irregularities or arrhythmias, for example —appropriate medications are dispensed.

The next steps in heart attack treatment almost all have to do with rest and relief of the anxieties and pressures caused by (or which perhaps were the cause of) the heart attack. This doesn't mean flat-on-the-back bed rest in most cases, but probably includes sitting up in bed, resting in a bedside chair, or safe and not overtaxing physical activity.

Much of this medical attention may take place in an intensive care unit (ICU) or a specialized cardiac care unit (CCU). In so-called uncomplicated heart attack cases, a few days in the ICU or CCU may be followed by as few as three to four days or as many as two weeks of rest, convalescence, observation, and medical management on the regular hospital floors or separate convalescent areas before release to the home. Those with continuing heart and circulatory complications may need longer hospital stays, possibly including time spent recovering from heart surgery.

Two to three months after an uncomplicated attack, life should be back to normal. Sometimes people confine themselves to a life of *post*-heart attack invalidism even when they are capable of leading *pre*-heart attack existences. This is a psychological depression; these folks see themselves as damaged goods, afraid to move a muscle for fear of another, potentially death-dealing attack. These people may be creating self-fulfilling prophesies. By dwelling on the dark and morbid, by refraining from activities that promote health and vitality and quality of life, they are surely speeding the end of their lives. Life is meant to be lived, and if the style of that life—physical activity, diet, psychological outlook—is a healthy one, there is no reason why a first attack cannot be the only heart attack, and eventually an event of the distant past.

Q: **What is streptokinase? I hear it's a miracle drug for people with heart attacks.**

A: Streptokinase—as the ''ase'' ending indicates—is an enzyme. And some studies show that if administered properly and very soon after a heart attack (more effective if given within four to six hours after onset), it seems that it not only can keep heart muscle damage to a minimum, but also may very well save your life. Some research supports the conclusion that a clot-busting drug is of some value even if given within 18 hours after onset of a heart attack.

What streptokinase does is to ''lyse'' the thrombosis; that is, it disintegrates the blood clot blocking the artery to the heart. The quicker the introduction of streptokinase into the attack sufferer's system via cardiac catheterization, the quicker the lyse, and the smaller and less damaging the infarcted area of the heart.

That's what some studies show. Others show the opposite—that streptokinase doesn't work miracles in the fight against death, and that a lot of its benefit is caused more by its action as a vasodilator over the long haul than as a blockage buster at the start.

Q:

Are there any other clot-busting drugs around?

A:

Yes, but . . .

Q:

But what?

A:

A British study—believed to be the largest ever conducted to evaluate the treatment of heart attacks—was the very first to directly compare all the drugs used to dissolve blood clots when a person is having a heart attack. Researchers found that all three drugs are equally effective in saving lives but that the oldest and cheapest —streptokinase—is the safest.

Streptokinase costs about $200 per treatment, as against $2,200 to $2,700 for T.P.A., the most expensive. Yet in their belief that more expensive means better, doctors in American hospitals do not use streptokinase nearly as much. The third drug, Eminase, costs $1,700 per treatment.

As to effectiveness, about 90 percent of patients receiving each drug survived, and the study found no major differences in heart function among those treated with the three drugs. However, a potentially devastating complication of clot-busting drug treatment is bleeding, and T.P.A. and Eminase caused a small but statistically significant greater number of strokes from bleeding into the brain than did streptokinase.

Q: Why is it important to keep the infarcted area small?

A: Because death is a natural result of too big an infarct. What happens is that when the infarcted area becomes necrotic—that is, when the cells die from lack of oxygen—or even are severely damaged, scar tissue forms. In an uncomplicated heart attack, the scar tissue does not impair the heart's normal functions, and life goes on.

However, if the heart attack was serious and the scar large, it *does* get in the way. So much so that heart failure and congestive heart failure may occur, and a large bulge caused by a **ventricular aneurysm** may appear, causing life-threatening conditions that might require surgery.

Q: Are there any new treatments—maybe in the developmental or experimental stage—for dissolving clots during heart attacks?

A: In late-1991 University of Miami doctors stopped a heart attack in progress by threading a laser catheter through the victim's arteries and disintegrating the fatty deposit that had blocked the flow of blood in a coronary artery. This case was the first known instance where such a clot-dissolving technique was used *during* an actual heart attack.

And as a matter of fact, the University of Miami is one of 30 medical centers nationwide testing the use of lasers to clear blocked arteries in the heart as a preventive measure.

Eduardo DeMarchena, director of interventional cardiology for the University of Miami School of Medicine, said the procedure—while unlikely to replace clot-dissolving drugs, which are cheaper and easier to administer—could someday become a routine alternative for heart attack patients who cannot be treated with the drugs.

Q: **So once the clot is dissolved, then everything's all right again?**

A: Not quite. Let's say a clot has been dissolved, leaving the coronary artery open to send oxygenated blood to the gasping heart. That's great—except that quite often the capillaries that feed the deeper recesses of the heart muscle don't benefit, blood doesn't end up going there, and the heart muscle doesn't end up functioning all that well.

Besides, clots form in portions of arteries that are narrowed by the accumulation of atherosclerotic plaque deposits. Without eliminating those deposits—and there aren't many easy ways to do that—a new clot is ripe for forming at the very spot where the first one was dissolved.

Streptokinase works about three-fourths of the time. But if dissolving the clot makes any difference in the course of the disease, it hasn't been proven yet.

Q: Can you have more than one heart attack at a time?

A: Generally you have only one at a time, but it may be one in a rapidly occurring series. In fact, the one you feel, the one that hits you hard and puts you down, may be merely the most recent attack in a string of them. Moreover, symptoms you feel now may be just the tail end of a weeks-long attack made up of a steady buildup.

Also, a new heart attack may come right on the heels (within a couple of weeks) of a previous one, and the infarcted area may be the same. What usually isn't the same is the outcome—this new heart attack (called an extension of infarction) can lead to grave, even fatal, complications. And according to one study, 30 percent of those people with myocardial infarctions suffer an extension of infarction within the first day or two after the previous attack.

Q: Do hearts stop during heart attacks?

A: No. Only those suffering cardiac arrest do. The heart's electrical system going crazy or heartbeat irregularities like ventricular fibrillation lead to the often fatal cardiac arrest.

Q: **What are the chances of surviving a heart attack?**

A: With no or few complications, you have about an 80 to 90 percent chance of surviving the attack. With complications, the chance of dying zooms to 60 percent and higher. Unfortunately, many people have these complications; of the 1.5 million people who suffer heart attacks in the United States each year, statistics show that only about half survive.

Q: **How can I prevent a heart attack from happening or prevent a second one from happening?**

A: As we've said before, heart disease is a multifactorial thing. It's also difficult to say firmly and with unimpeachable conviction that if you do this and that and such, you'll never have a heart attack or never experience another one.

But it seems that nearly every health and medical expert around will agree that change for the better in life-style, and controlling the basic risk factors—smoking, drinking, serum cholesterol, stress, poor physical fitness, diabetes, high blood pressure—will go a long way toward making your heart a happier and healthier one.

More details and tips can be found in the section on prevention in this book.

Q: Is it safe to have sexual relations after a heart attack?

A: Better after than during. The answer, seriously, is yes. So many people avoid resuming their sex life, fearful that their heart won't take the rigors of intercourse and they'll have a blow-out and expire in a blaze of glory. Not so, in general. Walking up the stairs from the basement to the second floor bedroom in the average house elevates the heart rate more than sex does in 70 to 80 percent of the middle age men who have had uncomplicated heart attacks. Wait about a month or so before returning to those more pleasant moments. Talk it over with your physician or therapy counselor. It's nothing to be ashamed about.

The greatest problem in post-heart attack sex is not physical but psychological—fear of sudden death (despite assurances of safety), psychosomatic impotence, and fear and concern transferred from spouse or sexual partner to the heart attack sufferer. It is reported that of all people alive today who have had heart attacks, sexual activity has decreased or stopped altogether in 58 to 75 percent of them. What's worse, 66 to 87 percent of heart attack sufferers state that their doctors never gave them information about sexual activity, post-attack.

Therapy—group or private—may be required and clearly can be helpful.

Q: Do heart attacks run in the family?

A: If you mean "Is a heart attack a genetic problem?" then indications do point to a family link. There have been a number of studies performed over the years, and they all, to one extent or another, show that if you are a first-degree relative (for instance, a child) of someone who suffered a heart attack around or before the age of 50, your chance of having a heart attack is significantly increased. One study puts that chance at two-to-four times greater than in those whose parent or parents (but usually the father) had heart attacks early in life. All of this family history seems to apply more to men than women.

What this means is that if your father had a heart attack, your risk is greater, and that if your brother is having heart problems, you should probably have yourself checked. What it does not mean, necessarily, is that you are *certain* to have a heart attack. If you control the controllable risk factors—especially that of high cholesterol levels in the blood, and especially if you begin controlling them at an early age—you may beat the odds.

Q: Is it true that heart attacks in women are on the rise? Why?

A: Unfortunately, it seems to be true. Heart attack is the number one killer of American women; and in the U.S. all cardiovascular diseases

combined claim nearly 500,000 women's lives annually. (All forms of cancer combine to kill about 222,000 women annually.) For the longest time, heart attacks among women were rare— so rare, in fact, that little research has been performed looking into why women are less susceptible than men. Genes, less of the male hormone testosterone, life-style— all could be important factors.

What is known about the rise in female heart attacks is that as more women enter the previously male-dominated worlds of business and industry, they are also affected by the stress and tension, unnatural work conditions, bad food eaten hastily, and lack of exercise their male counterparts take for granted. Most significant of all, according to a study headed by researchers at Boston University School of Medicine, is the rise in female smokers. For women under the age of 50 who smoke a pack-and-a-half a day or more, the chance of having a heart attack is 10 times greater than among women who have never smoked. About 65 percent of the heart attacks were traced back to cigarette smoking, a habit that can be stopped to avoid a disaster that is almost certainly preventable.

Still, far fewer women have heart attacks than men, and the incidence of coronary heart disease in women is less than in men. But after menopause, women's heart disease risk grows. Estrogen, or rather the lack of it, is the factor operating here. In the largest study to date— published in a September 1991 *New England Journal of Medicine*—authorities found that estrogen replacement after menopause cut the risk of major coronary disease by 44 percent and coronary mortality by 39 percent. A question left unanswered by the study was how soon after starting estrogen would a woman see the benefits of a reduction in heart disease. But on a precautionary note, other experts warn that hormone therapy should not be used indiscriminately among women at high risk for breast or endometrial cancers.

Q: **Is the heart attack rate among men rising or falling?**

A: A study of workers for the Du Pont Corporation during the years from 1957 through 1983—and in some years the employee population reached 108,000 people—showed this: From 1957 to 1959, the first-time heart attack rate among male employees was 3.19 per 1,000; by 1981 to 1983, that figure had dropped to 2.29 per 1,000. That's a significant drop of 28.2 percent, and mostly attributed to life-style changes and elimination of risk factors. In addition, during the early years of the study, men between 45 and 54 years of age had a heart attack rate of 6.47 per 1,000; by the 1980s, the very same age group's heart attack rate had plummeted to 2.83 per 1,000.

Even now, some years after the study, researchers and scientists feel that these Du Pont figures probably mirror what's happening in the society at large.

Q: Did the heart attack rate go down among all categories of male workers?

A: As a matter of fact, and interestingly enough, no. Among salaried—that is, white-collar workers—the first-time heart attack rate dropped 37 percent. Among hourly-pay—or blue-collar workers—the heart attack rate also dropped, but only by 18 percent, or about half as much. One reason could be the stress caused by fear of making less or the loss of work hours and thus earnings among the blue-collar group. Another reason may be that workers with higher educational levels—presumably this refers to the white-collar group—are more likely to effect life-style changes to reduce risks, like stopping smoking, eating better, exercising regularly, or other changes that may or may not be within the power or financial picture of blue-collar workers to change.

A discouraging P.S. to this Du Pont study: Despite the reduction in first-time heart attacks, there was very little increase in the survival rate of those who did have the heart attacks. In the early days of the study, 30 percent of heart attack victims died within a month; today that number is 24 percent. A drop, but a small one.

All of which says clearly that the route to take is a life-style-changing, preventive one.

Q:
I've heard that having a vasectomy increases your chances of having a heart attack. True?

A:
False. The best study undertaken to examine the supposed link between vasectomy and heart attack—a cooperative venture of medical groups in the Boston and Seattle areas—showed that nonfatal myocardial infarctions among 4,733 vasectomized men was 1.3 cases per 1,000 man years (the number of men multiplied by the period of time they were studied). This rate was just about identical to that for men who had not undergone vasectomies. As the study concluded: " . . . [The] risk of acute myocardial infarction is not increased in men (up to and including 15 years) after vasectomy. Since long-term effects have not yet been excluded altogether, we will continue to follow our vasectomized men indefinitely."

Q:
I've heard that taking aspirin regularly is a way of avoiding heart attacks. Does it work?

A:
The idea behind aspirin-taking being a heart attack preventive comes from the scientific feeling that aspirin keeps platelets (small cells) in the blood from lumping together and forming clots. No clots, no blocked blood path, no infarct, and ergo, no problem. There is a problem, though: Studies exist for both sides of the issue, each promoting a different theory, proposing varying doses, and claiming or

disclaiming therapeutic properties for men or women or both or neither. And all the studies hedged a bit in their declarations and recommended further research to pin down the facts. It's enough to give a person a good reason to reach for an aspirin—to get rid of the headache caused by reading all this stuff.

Aspirin as protective got a big boost from a 1983 Veterans Administration study that looked at how and if aspirin might affect the heart attack death rate among men with unstable angina. (Aspirin's protective role in women is uncertain, and wasn't studied.) The researchers used a buffered aspirin preparation to avoid causing gastrointestinal problems. What they found when they compared an aspirin-taking group with a placebo-taking group was that the aspirin-takers had 51 percent fewer heart attacks, plus a reduction in mortality among those who did have heart attacks.

Another big boost for the value of aspirin therapy came in 1988. At that time, results of a major national study provided compelling evidence that aspirin can help control the national epidemic of heart attacks, according to the American Heart Association. In light of this, though, the group continues to caution against indiscriminate use of the widely available drug and reminds that aspirin therapy does nothing to eradicate underlying arterial disease.

Yet another large national study—this one reported in the *Annals of Internal Medicine* in mid-1991—concluded that alternate-day, low-dosage aspirin therapy greatly reduces the risk of a first heart attack among people with chronic stable angina, a group at high risk for cardiovascular death. And in findings presented at the annual meeting of the American College of Cardiology in 1991, researchers at Oxford University in England underscored the results of more than 200 studies of aspirin. These studies, said the Oxford team, provide conclusive evidence that aspirin can cut the risk of a second heart attack or stroke by 25 percent.

Clearly, this entire issue is one to discuss with your physician or other health-care practitioner.

Q: Besides smoking, what are the major heart attack risk factors for women?

A: One is what is called ''surgical menopause''— **bilateral oophorectomy** (removal of both ovaries) at the same time a hysterectomy is performed. Harvard Medical School researchers found that women who underwent surgical menopause had a much higher incidence of heart attacks, and the chance of having a heart attack increased as the age of the woman at surgery decreased. In other words, a woman undergoing bilateral oophorectomy at a young age—say, 35 years old—had a far greater chance of having an attack than someone older having the operation. The researchers also determined that early natural menopause wasn't a heart attack risk, unless menopause occurred before the woman was 35.

Oral contraceptives are also implicated in increased risk of myocardial infarctions, affecting cholesterol and blood pressure levels, among other things. And even if a woman has stopped taking the pill, her chances of a heart attack are greater than women who have never taken the pill; the risk is directly proportional to how long the woman took the pill before stopping its use: A woman who took the pill for 10 or more years has about a two-and-a-half times greater chance of heart attack than someone who took it for less than five years.

Q: Does everybody who has a heart attack go into intensive care or cardiac care units?

A: Nearly all do, but according to a Yale University School of Medicine study, more than a third of heart attack sufferers don't need to. And by keeping them out of ICUs or CCUs, each patient could save a great deal of money—ICU accommodations are about three times as expensive as regular hospital rooms.

Cardiac care units are overused and, it seems in many cases, under-useful. Studies show that very little care happens there that couldn't happen in regular rooms and wards, that despite all the expensive tests and drugs there is little or no difference in mortality rates between CCUs and regular rooms, and that often people do better recovering from a heart attack at home than in a CCU. In fact, the evidence from at least one study indicates that, in some circumstances, you can be better treated at home (1) if you are elderly and without **hypotension** (abnormally low blood pressure), heart failure, or persistent pain; (2) if the heart attack is uncomplicated and you are seen by a physician some hours after the incident; or (3) if your home is far from the hospital and you want care at home.

"Our current strategy of forcing all patients into the same kind of high-technology expensive care is hardly defensible," wrote Sam C. Eggertsen, M.D., and Alfred O. Berg, M.D., M.P.H., of the University of Washington School of Medicine, in the *Journal of the American Medical Association*. "It deserves much more critical scrutiny."

Q: Are there any other "miracle drugs" for fighting heart attacks?

A: Well, miraculous is a concept best left with religion (which medical science is not, no matter how doctors behave). But there are a few items that seem, in medical lingo, to be very encouraging.

We've discussed one type before: calcium channel blockers, used for angina pectoris. These drugs block calcium from entry into the heart cells, calcium being a primary agent in causing coronary spasm, and coronary spasm being very dangerous indeed.

Another category of drug is the **beta blocker**, which is used commonly as an antihypertensive medication, as well as for arrhythmias and angina. Beta blockers keep the sympathetic nervous system, which controls heartbeat, in check. By slowing the pressure, beta blockers are able to keep infarct damage small. Beta blockers may even bestow an anti-heart attack preventive effect on people taking them for high blood pressure.

The big breakthrough beta blocker was propranolol—Inderal is the brand name for it—

which was so effective in a National Heart, Lung and Blood Institute trial study as a way to help attack sufferers survive and avoid second attacks that the study was called off nine months ahead of schedule because it would have been unethical not to give everybody the drug right away. It reduced mortality by 26 percent. The researchers weren't sure how propranolol worked. They were just thrilled to have it, and it is being used a lot today.

The latest news surrounds something called **tissue-type plasminogen activator**, a genetically-engineered enzyme once thought to work almost twice as well in dissolving clots as streptokinase. Now known to work only as well as streptokinase, it is significantly more expensive.

Q: How soon after a heart attack is it safe to start exercising?

A: Depending on your doctor's viewpoint, you may be up and doing some sort of exercise very soon after your heart attack. Exercise, either in the hospital or after release when you get home, or both, is useful in a number of ways: It helps to bring to the surface any underlying, continuing heart problems; it can aid in forming a better prognosis (including determining if you are a candidate for surgery); it prevents muscle deconditioning that occurs during long bed-bound stays in the hospital; one Harvard Medical School/Boston School of Nursing study showed in laboratory animals that exercise soon after a heart attack, during the healing phase, causes the scar tissue to become thinner; and exercise is good for mental outlook, for building confidence, and for chasing away post-attack depression.

What is unclear is whether exercise right after a myocardial infarction is important in preventing another one.

Q: **Do heart attacks happen at certain times more than others? More often during the day? At night?**

A: If you have a history of heart disease, the occurrence is spread out evenly, with perhaps a slight rise at night.

Oddly, if you don't have a history of heart disease, beware of Mondays. In a 32-year University of Manitoba study of 4,000 men, the worst, most common day for having a fatal heart attack was Monday.

No one knows for sure why that is—might have something to do with the stress of returning to work after an easy weekend, or sudden re-exposure to toxic chemicals.

CORONARY ARTERY DISEASE

Q: What can you tell us about coronary artery disease?

A: In a sense, it's already been told in previous pages. The coronary arteries, which bring blood to the heart itself for its own needs, may become clogged with deposits on the artery walls that are associated with atherosclerosis (from **atheroma**, meaning a fatty mass, covered by fibrous substance, and existing as a plaque in an artery wall; and **sclerosis**, a hardening) and lead to total occlusion. There are several hypotheses concerning how and why athero-sclerosis grows fatty deposits in the artery walls; none has been confirmed.

The acceleration of atherosclerosis and, thus, coronary artery disease may be checked by being careful to control what are called risk factors, actions or conditions that have been found to worsen the condition. The primary risk factors for coronary artery disease, as mentioned before, are cigarette smoking, high cholesterol levels, high blood pressure, stress, lack of exercise, and diabetes. A family history of the disease and being a male are two other risk factors that, unlike the others, aren't changeable (sex change operations won't do it).

More detailed information about these risk factors, and how you can eliminate them from your life, can be found in the section on prevention, which appears later in this book.

We've already looked into the most common manifestations of coronary artery disease—angina pectoris and heart attacks at the top of the list—and the way they are being treated through use of drugs. But these days, surgery to correct the problem is becoming almost a casual event. About 350,000 people a year or more are having coronary bypass graft surgery, at an average cost of $37,000 per operation (30 percent to physicians, 70 percent to hospitals), making it a nearly $13 billion growth industry. Its use has been seen as an aid to the quality of life for coronary artery disease sufferers; yet it is under fire from experts who claim it is overprescribed, no panacea, and doesn't enable people to live longer lives.

In the next section, we'll look at what bypass surgery is, what its proponents and critics and their respective studies are saying, and what the alternatives are, including the most controversial of all: chelation therapy.

But before we turn to those pages, here are some sobering statistics to remember about coronary artery disease:

• There is one coronary artery disease-related death in America every minute. By the time you finish this page, at least one person will have died.

• There are more than six million people with diagnosed coronary artery disease—and perhaps millions more who have it but have no symptoms . . . yet.

• The annual price tag in 1991 for coronary artery disease was somewhere around $101 billion.

3 BYPASS AND THE ALTERNATIVES

Q: What happens during a bypass operation? What gets bypassed?

A: In this procedure, which was developed back in the mid-1960s, a vein is removed (or "harvested," as the medicos like to say) from the person's leg, possibly the thigh, and is used as a detour around the blocked portion of the affected coronary artery (or arteries—often as many as three or four may be bypassed): One end is sewn into the aorta and the other into the coronary artery down the line from the obstruction, allowing free flow of blood. Another bypass method is one in which the internal mammary artery, which carries blood to the chest wall and other structures, is linked up with the coronary artery to end-around the blockage. Many experts consider this method the graft of choice for most patients with extensive coronary disease, although it, too, has some limitations.

For years surgeons have searched for a synthetic material that could be used, but so far no satisfactory substitutes for human tissue grafts have been found.

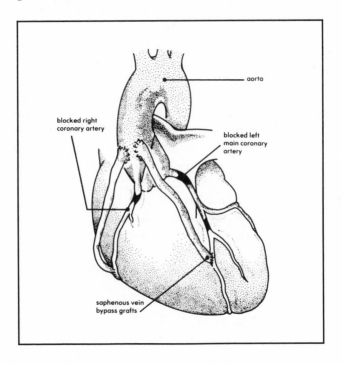

Q: Is there any age limit for getting a bypass?

A: It seems not. Study after study indicates that while bypass in its early years had a less than glowing operative mortality record on older people (around 13 percent), it's probably down to about 5 percent or less now. True, while mortality rates for this procedure have fallen steadily since its invention—current literature notes that overall operative mortality of 0 to 3 percent can be achieved with current techniques—it is best to remember that, as for all surgeries, mortality rises with age, with the number and severity of coexistent diseases, and with the presence of any medical problems that are likely to be adversely affected by anesthesia. It is also best to bear in mind that this overall mortality rate of 0 to 3 percent reflects the results with carefully selected patients in the best centers. And mortality increases with the number of vessels replaced.

Nevertheless, writing in the November 15, 1991, issue of the *American Journal of Cardiology*, a Cleveland Clinic cardiologist says that age alone is no reason to deny heart patients in their 80s the potential relief and added life that bypass surgery offers. He studied the records of nearly 200 people over 80 who had had either angioplasty or bypass surgery and found that their survival and complications rates were similar to those of younger people having the same operations.

Most people in various studies who received bypasses claimed that their angina was gone or much improved. Five-year survival following surgery, even in patients over 65, can be as high as 96.9 percent. However, it is worth noting that at 10-year follow-up in one of the largest studies conducted, there was no statistical significance between survival and medical treatment or survival with surgical treatment except for certain subgroups of patients who quite clearly did far better with surgical than with medical treatment.

Recurrence of angina, to a similar or lesser extent, does occur among elderly coronary bypass patients, and so does the need in some cases for reoperation due to atherosclerotic growth in the newly grafted blood vessels.

Clearly, bypass is not something to be entered into lightly, without lots of information and second and even third opinions—no matter your age.

Q: **Men and women seem to differ greatly when it comes to heart disease. Are they different when it comes to bypass surgery, too?**

A: The evidence points that way. But in this case, the women come out on the short end of the scalpel. According to researchers, being a woman is the third greatest risk factor involved in death from bypass surgery, coming right after older age and having a 90 percent or better obstruction of the left main coronary artery.

Fewer women than men have bypass operations. According to the American Heart Association, of the 353,000 bypass operations performed in 1988, only 23.5 percent (or 82,955) were performed on women. And while it used to be predominantly premenopausal women who had the surgery, it's now just the opposite. Women tend to have more one- and two-vessel disease (that is, one or two obstructed coronary arteries) and less three-vessel disease than men.

Q: What are some of the more serious side effects of bypass surgery?

A: There have been reports that some people are experiencing conduction problems, some as serious as complete heart block, and nobody's quite sure why.

Quite as serious, and more prevalent, is damage to the brain and memory. Whether long- or short-term, it seems to happen frequently enough to worry many medical researchers. On one end of the worry scale are those who recognize that after bypass surgery many patients have difficulty concentrating and remembering and suffer an I.Q. drop. But they contend that it is usually temporary and usually clears up in a couple of months. At the other end of the "postoperative cognitive impairment" scale are people like Hal Lear, M.D., whose unsuccessful fight against heart disease—and his wife's journal of the struggle—became public in the book and made-for-television movie "Heartsounds." Lear's three years after bypass surgery were times of mental torture, with a crippled memory that forgot names and places. In a Cleveland Clinic study, 12 percent of bypass patients had memory loss or other brain malfunctions for short or long periods.

Preliminary results of an international study show that bypass surgery produces subtle, long-lasting impairment of mental performance in nearly one in five people who undergo the procedure. These findings, however, are still under review.

Why does this happen? Well, it seems to be a problem attending all open heart surgeries, not just bypass operations. Some of the guesses center around the heart-lung machine and what happens to the blood when it is circulated away from the body, through the machine, then back into the body. Some investigators suggest it has to do with the tubes the blood passes through— they could have bits of contamination or they may generate tiny bubbles that get into the brain —or perhaps it's something called "protein sludging." Others think that atherosclerotic plaque breaks off from the arteries and floats to the brain. Whatever it is, it happens, and many physicians don't know about it or don't tell prospective bypass and open-heart surgery patients about it.

Stroke, during or immediately following the operation, rose from about 0.57 percent to 2.4 percent over the five-year period 1979 to 1983, largely due to the rising age of patients being operated on. A 1988 study showed a risk of 2.9 percent for patients who had a prior history of stroke and had general anesthesia for *any* surgery. Other studies have found similar stroke rates and found that the probability of stroke correlates very highly with increasing age of those having bypass surgery.

Another mentally related bypass result is the kind of depression and unfounded fear that causes one to become an invalid, similar to what we saw among heart attack survivors. Despite the rosy picture painted by many of the strongest proponents of bypass surgeries—those who developed the procedure, built their reputations on it, and make most of their money from it— a large percentage of bypass recipients never go back to work even though their pain is reduced. Further, they become sexually inactive and think of themselves as damaged goods. Those in the worst shape psychologically after the

operation are those who were in the worst
shape physically before the operation; they thus
had a long time to develop a lousy self-image
and depressed attitude, which even obvious
improvement can't eliminate. Some doctors use
this psychological angle to rush people into
bypass surgery, the rationale being that the
sooner the operation, the shorter the time
beforehand to dwell on diminished capabilities.
Also, those with good jobs and high status tend
to return to work more often than those with
low-status jobs. Whether this has to do with
white-collar workers who can resume desk work
versus blue-collar workers afraid or unable to
do lifting and pulling is uncertain, but possible.

Other side effects or complications include
infections at the chest incision and on the leg at
the site of the stripped vein.

Q: Who should undergo bypass surgery?

A: There are some who believe nobody should,
and we'll get to those people soon.

But in general, physicians believe that people
with angina so severe that they can barely move
without an attack are prime candidates, as are
those with serious narrowing of the left main
coronary artery, no matter if the symptoms are
serious or not, because the person is at risk of
sudden death or heart attack. The narrowing can
be determined through coronary angiography.
Many surgeons go ahead with bypass operations
if the person has only mild or moderate angina
symptoms and two or three coronary arteries
narrowed with atherosclerotic deposits.

It is felt by these physicians and researchers that longevity is increased and quality of life is improved by having a bypass under those circumstances. A too-diseased ventricle may militate against a bypass; however, if it's not too damaged, according to Michael Debakey, M.D., "there is a 75 percent chance of improvements, though probably not a return to normal."

Sometimes, though, people don't fall into neat categories, or readings don't give clear-cut answers. Then, it's up to your doctor or the second- or third-opinion physician you visit.

And when you get a second opinion, get it from a surgeon who also does alternative procedures such as balloon angioplasty (although it, too, has come under fire from critics who say that too many are performed unnecessarily). Otherwise you may end up getting only a confirmed cutter's point of view. Further, according to many leading experts, getting a second opinion on whether cardiac catheterization is necessary is the best way to protect yourself from an unnecessary bypass. You see—so goes their logic—once a person consents to having a cardiac catheterization, odds are that *something* amiss will be found and that bypass or balloon angioplasty will be recommended.

Q: Once you've had a bypass, do the new blood vessels stay clear and free for the rest of your life?

A: Afraid not. Even in successful cases, the new vessel or vessels may close, requiring more surgery. The metabolic factors that caused atherosclerosis in the original arteries to begin with are probably still present—bypass doesn't cure the disease, it alleviates the symptoms— and this is certainly so if diet, smoking, and other life-style changes aren't initiated.

The disturbing post-bypass statistics are that 10 years after the operation about 40 percent of grafted veins are totally clogged up again, and 50 percent of those not shut off are narrowed. (A Vanderbilt University Medical Center study found blockage of one degree or another in every single grafted vein seen in autopsies of 46 people who'd had bypass one to 14 years before.) Further, the progression of coronary artery disease is not influenced by surgery, and the incidence of angina pectoris even five years after surgery has been reported in up to 35 percent of patients, according to a 1988 report in the journal *Circulation*.

This is serious not only because of the recurrence of anginal pain, but because a second bypass operation to undo the failing first is technically much more difficult, the chance of death during or soon after the operation is greater, and the relief of angina symptoms— seemingly so dramatic after the first operation —are far less so after the second. In fact, a nine-year study of 200 repeat bypass operations, reported in the *American Journal of Cardiology*, found that reoperation is effective but carries an increased and immediate operative risk.

Indeed, there is evidence that even the very act of the bypass operation may cause acceleration of atherosclerosis. While this may be a risk that needs to be taken in the most necessary of bypass operations, a study from the departments of medicine and preventive medicine at the University of California at Los Angeles underscored the atherosclerotic danger of bypassing coronary arteries with minimal narrowing, defined as less than 50 percent narrowing of the artery. This study looked at 85 men who had had a graft of some of their coronary arteries but not all. After three years, the researchers found that the "progression of atherosclerosis . . . was more than 10 times as frequent (38 percent versus 3 percent) in bypassed arteries with minimal atherosclerosis as in comparable arteries that were not bypassed." Their conclusion: " . . . Minimally diseased coronary arteries should not be bypassed."

Q: **Why is bypass surgery as expensive as it is?**

A: No good reason. At bypass's very beginnings, sure, it was a risky operation that took a lot of time, and the costs reflected that. Today, though, bypasses are done practically assembly-line fashion in some places, and it's relatively safe and relatively quick (lasting anywhere from three to five hours). Yet the cost is the same as it was back then. Such operations—and there are others that have followed the same pattern—are known in the trade as "winners." The losers are us.

Some of the statistics on bypass break down thusly: Since 1968 there have been approximately one million bypass procedures performed at a total cost of tens of billions of dollars. In 1976 there were 80,000 procedures at an annual cost of $960 million. In 1981 there were 160,000 procedures at an annual cost of $3.2 billion. And in 1988 there were 353,000 procedures at an annual cost of $10 billion.

By the early 1990s the median cost of a bypass operation was $37,000, including $4,800 for cardiac catheterization—at an annual expenditure of $13 billion. (And, in fact, we should also mention that there has been a 300 percent increase in the number of cardiac catheterizations performed since 1979—from 290,000 that year to more than 900,000 in 1988.)

As you can see, the bypass business is booming. The advent of bypass surgery rescued the fortunes of cardiac surgeons, who had been hurting, relatively speaking, until it arrived on the scene, and it allowed hospitals to expand both their facilities and their coffers.

Of all the problems and controversies surrounding bypass, cost—the fact that it is a $13 billion a year industry—is somewhere near the top. Many people, though, don't care. Insurance covers their bills, and, anyway, their health is worth any price. But we all end up paying that insurance bill through increased premiums. And it hurts doubly if that surgery wasn't necessary in the first place. In recent years Rand Corporation and other leading researchers have come down hard on bypass surgery. Reviewing hundreds of such procedures at three hospitals in 1979, 1980, and 1982, Rand concluded that only 56 percent were clearly appropriate. In this esteemed research center's analysis, 30 percent were done for "equivocal" reasons and 14 percent for "inappropriate" reasons, according to a 1988 report in the *Journal of the American Medical Association*.

Q: Will my health insurance pay for my bypass surgery?

A: Good policies will. However, even good policies may not cover the cost of rehabilitation programs, or exercise programs, after a certain amount of time. It's well worth your while to check into such things now, before any problems pop up.

Q: Will having a bypass after a heart attack prevent future heart attacks?

A: No. Most good studies show that those who receive a bypass after a heart attack have as great a risk of having another attack as those heart attack sufferers who don't have a bypass, and the bypass recipient doesn't live any longer either.

As to whether a preventive bypass will avert a first heart attack: maybe yes, maybe no. Don't bet on it.

Q: What portion of the population gets the most bypasses?

A: White males. Even though more blacks than whites get disabling angina earlier in life, 97 percent of bypass operations in the U.S. are performed on whites. A cynic might suggest that money has something to do with this state of unfair affairs.

That same cynic might also note with no astonishment that bypass is performed in the U.S. twice as much in Canada and Australia, and four times as much as in Western Europe, even though the heart disease demographics in all four places are generally the same.

Q: What are the alternatives to bypass operations?

A: They fall into three general categories: (1) medication therapy, (2) lightly invasive procedures, specifically balloon angioplasty and experimental laser angioplasty, and (3) the controversial chelation therapy.

Let's take medication for starters.

MEDICATION

Q: Is drug-taking a viable alternative to bypass?

A: One of the most complete and important studies about bypass ever undertaken gave a resounding yes to that question.

The Coronary Artery Surgery Study (CASS), sponsored by the National Heart, Lung and Blood Institute, was released some years back, and, despite the sniping by vested interest critics, it was a bombshell and a trailblazer for a new direction in bypass and medication use.

CASS looked at 780 people who either had mild angina or had just a heart attack but no subsequent angina. The study compared those who underwent bypass surgery with those who were only treated medically. What it found was that there was no significant difference in mortality or in the occurrence of heart attacks between people who had surgery and people who were treated solely with medication. The study said that people with mild angina or recent heart attacks with no angina could put off thoughts of bypass until the day came, if ever, when their condition had deteriorated to the point where they needed surgery—with no health penalty for the delay.

The importance is clear: Serious surgery can be postponed if not avoided altogether; health costs are reduced (nonbypass-related drugs are on average more expensive than bypass-related maintenance drugs, but there's no $37,000 surgery fee); and while 23.7 percent of those in the study who took only medicine eventually had surgery (at a rate of 4.7 percent a year over five years), the delay was sufficiently long that had they had bypass when it was first recommended, they might already have been having a second round of bypasses along with greater mortality risk. This danger was avoided. Said Eugene Passamani, M.D., of the CASS study, "In postponing surgery as long as possible (and avoiding having to chance a second bypass), it becomes a question of having your one good operation at the best possible time."

The CASS study also said that while surgery doesn't add years to recipients' lives, it may

provide greater angina relief, require less anti-
anginal medication, and reduce pain during
exercise better than medication therapy. On the
other hand, these benefits of surgery—so-called
quality of life factors—didn't cause bypass
recipients to have more leisure-time fun or to
get back to work any better than the medication
group. And bypass should be restricted to cases
of 70 percent or greater blockage of the left
main coronary artery (only about 1.5 percent of
cases) and debilitating angina that doesn't
respond to medical treatment. Bypass should
not be used on people with no or mild symptoms
who have a blockage in only one coronary artery.

Q: **Which are the drugs used instead of bypass?**

A: Some of our old standbys: nitroglycerin and
other nitrates, calcium channel blockers, and
especially beta blockers.

BALLOON ANGIOPLASTY

Q: How does a balloon help my coronary
arteries? What's the procedure?

A: The true medical name for the balloon
procedure that is now being performed 150,000
times a year in place of bypass surgery is

percutaneous transluminal coronary angioplasty—PTCA for short.

In PTCA—developed by Swiss doctor Andreas R. Gruentzig and first used in the United States in 1977, a decade after the introduction of bypass—a plastic catheter tube with a tiny balloon at its forward tip is inserted into the groin area and is delicately pushed through the femoral artery and on toward the heart until it almost literally bumps into the coronary artery blockage. At that point the balloon is inflated; in effect, it squeezes or mashes the obstruction up against the artery wall to clear a path for blood to resume traveling along. And that's it. No chest scar, no stripped leg, no open heart. And the figure for the number of people who can have PTCA instead of bypass is at least 20 percent, and some excited doctors put the figure as high as 50 to 60 percent. In some instances, especially after a heart attack, streptokinase is used in combination with balloon angioplasty to clear the arteries even better.

We should point out, however, that PTCA has its share of critics. A large National Institutes of Health study of patients with acute myocardial infarction suggests that 40 percent of angioplasties are unnecessary, with the researchers concluding that in many cases angioplasty can be safely deferred until patients have recurrent ischemia.

Q: **How long does it take to recover from a PTCA operation?**

A: Most people who have uncomplicated PTCAs are up and around the very next day and are probably home the day after that.

Q: **How much does PTCA cost?**

A: In PTCA not only the balloon is inflated. The cost is probably around $10,000—although that favorably compares to the $37,000 or more for bypass; the hospital stay is two days compared to bypass's eight or more days.

Q: **How does the PTCA success rate compare with bypass? And how about complications and setbacks?**

A: The San Francisco Heart Institute, an important and busy center for PTCA, provides these figures on the procedure. (Note: Figures will vary from hospital to hospital, depending on the expertise of those performing the procedure and on how often the procedure is done there.) The San Francisco study examined 300 PTCA patients and found that:

• Forty-three of the patients had had previous bypass surgery but were clogged up again, and PTCA was recommended.

• Despite the feeling among some M.D.'s that PTCA's value is limited to cases where only one coronary artery is involved, multiple angioplasty can be performed successfully. In such cases, the most occluded artery is "ballooned" first.

• Success in mashing the artery wall deposits is nearly 90 percent, and more than 92 percent of patients showed marked and noticeably healthier clinical readings.

• Fewer than 3 percent of the people suffered sudden side effects during the PTCA procedure serious enough to warrant emergency surgery. (Sometimes a spontaneous occlusion occurs during PTCA, and the person needs to be taken for immediate bypass surgery instead.)

• The mortality rate for PTCA is about the same or even less than for bypass—about 1 percent—although that, too, differs according to severity of disease and other factors.

• After 15 months, 80 percent of PTCA patients report no or much improved angina.

• Repeat angioplasty for arteries that clog up again is as safe or safer than repeat bypass. In San Francisco 40 people had a second or third PTCA, and 37 were successful.

• It is too hazardous to do a balloon angioplasty on a left main coronary artery, unless pulmonary or systemic diseases make the person a poor risk for bypass surgery.

• In a study at Atlanta's Emory University, it's also been determined that a small, relatively recent obstruction is best for a successful mashing. An old, hard, calcified clog can splinter, and tiny shards of hardened deposit can float through the bloodstream and wreak havoc by lodging in the brain or lungs.

• Re-stenosis—when the newly opened vessel becomes narrowed or constricted again—

remains a major problem, says a February 1991 review of the status of the procedure in the journal *Contemporary Internal Medicine*. However, research into strategies to inhibit restenosis is currently underway at the National Heart, Lung and Blood Institute and at the University of Washington.

• According to Texas cardiologists, PTCA is a safe and effective treatment for octogenarians with coronary artery disease. In a long-term study of patients whose mean age was 82.4 years, the percentage of patients who experienced no further cardiac events—such as death, heart attack, or bypass surgery—following PTCA was 81 percent after one year and 78 percent after three years.

Q: What about "preventive angioplasties"?

A: Forget it. Like so-called preventive bypass— used to prevent worse conditions that could crop up later on—preventive angioplasties (used in mild cases when obstructions are less than 60 percent) don't prevent anything. If you have atherosclerosis, all this supposedly preventive procedure does is postpone a worse blockage and set you up to have a second angioplasty or a bypass in the not-too-distant future. And besides, studies show that such preventive angioplasty increases the risk of a post-balloon heart attack.

Q: **Does PTCA hurt?**

A: Not much, and certainly not as much as bypass. There will be pain at the site of the tiny incision in the groin where the balloon-tipped tube is inserted, and there will be a feeling of discomfort when the balloon is inflated (you'll very likely be awake during this procedure). The insides of arteries are not supplied with nerve endings, so there is no sense of pain involved with the catheter tube snaking up to the obstruction.

Q: **Any other advice about balloon angioplasty?**

A: Yes: Go to experts. Not every doctor performing the procedure has long experience with it. If you are going to have PTCA, be certain the person performing it has done many of them (at least 100) and that the operation is taking place in a hospital with a reputation for being a center of PTCA activity and research—and which has a solid reputation as a bypass center, too. Angioplasty is simple, compared to bypass, but it's not easy, and things can and do go wrong: The artery can crack or be accidentally dissected; the heart can go into sudden arrhythmia; or the artery may go into spasm. Having a doctor and a skilled surgical team who have seen it all (or mostly all) doing your operation—instead of somebody who does PTCA only occasionally to keep in practice and supplement income—can be a lifesaver.

Also, every angioplasty patient has to be willing to be a bypass patient, because if complications occur, that's what you'll suddenly become, no questions asked.

LASER

Q: I've been reading in the papers about lasers being used to clear up clogged arteries and get rid of angina. What's the whole story?

A: The whole story isn't written yet. While **laser coronary angioplasty** is full of promise and may someday replace much PTCA (as well as some bypass operations not already given over to PTCA), it is still somewhat experimental in nature. The Food and Drug Administration has approved its use only in peripheral vessels and as an adjunct to balloon angioplasty.

The theory behind laser angioplasty is simple, straightforward, and familiar to those who understand balloon angioplasty: A catheter one-eighth of an inch in diameter is inserted into an artery and pushed forward to the coronary occlusion. At that point, instead of inflating a balloon, the doctor in charge zaps the fatty deposits clogging the blood path with an argon laser beam that disintegrates the blockage. The blasted fragments are sucked up by a tiny vacuum cleaner.

Proponents declare that laser angioplasty will do the trick cheaply, quickly (in experimental trials, arteries were totally or partially cleared in under five minutes), and with minimum pain, and people undergoing it without complications can expect to be out of the hospital in a day. In this way, it is favorably compared to PTCA, and is seen as better than bypass for many arterial conditions.

Q: **Okay, but is it safe? Won't the laser just burn up the whole artery?**

A: Again, it's too early to say what laser technology has in store for our clogged-up innards. In early human clinical tests, the results have been mixed. Most of the cases have ended up in bypass (some out of pure safety concerns for the patient, others because that was what was planned all along), and there have been instances of damage to and even perforation of the artery wall, although in at least one instance it was the catheter tube itself and not the laser that caused the injury.

A 1990 report in *Medical Tribune* quoted some surgeons, radiologists, and cardiologists who use laser angioplasty; they stated that the high hopes once held out for the technique are not being fulfilled. Specifically problematic, according to critics, are the high mishap rates.

Any procedure in early stages has rough times and experiences setbacks; statistics generally get better as more are performed. No doubt the kinks will be ironed out of laser angioplasty, too. But right now it's just not quite right.

SELF HELP

Q: I've read about how some man refused to have a bypass operation and cured himself, without doctors. Who was it, and how did he do it?

A: You're almost certainly referring to the late writer-editor-lecturer Norman Cousins who, at the age of 65, had a heart attack (he'd had a "silent attack" some years before). At the suggestion that he undergo bypass surgery, Cousins decided to put that idea on the back burner, over a low flame, and instead see if he couldn't bring himself around by slowing down his work pace, eating better, avoiding stress, and staying in intimate tete-a-tete with his body.

Cousins was in a position to trust this body buddy system: Not too many years before, he'd had faith in his own healing powers, the power of positive thinking, and the doctor-patient relationship and had beaten the odds (and startled the doctors) by recovering from a serious collagen deterioration called ankylosing spondelitis. That time, he had pushed fear out of the picture—it was an assassin of recovery—had buoyed his spirits by watching old "Candid Camera" programs and Marx Brothers movies, had taken megadoses of vitamin C, checked out of the hospital and into a hotel, and was lucky enough to have an understanding and helpful doctor. He got well.

The other time, after the heart attack, he applied many of the same principles, plus walking exercises and other approaches. He made tremendous progress, and in one year, while not back to normal and certainly not healed to pristine perfection, he was back at work, walking six miles a day, cholesterol level down, back to his tennis game. He found a way to bypass the bypass, or at least had postponed it for a long time while enjoying a high quality of life.

Now, not everyone can benefit from this course of action; maybe only Norman Cousins could. After all, as he told his doctors, "They were looking at the darndest healing machine ever wheeled into the UCLA hospital." He had experience and confidence on his side. He also had money and the kind of leisure time away from the job that a relatively monied life-style can buy. He was famous, so doctors treated him with respect. They gave him as much information as he desired.

If we all had such privileges, maybe more of us could avoid bypass or PTCA. Even without those privileges, perhaps we can. For more details about his struggles and victories over disease, we refer you to two of his books: *Anatomy of an Illness as Perceived by the Patient* and *The Healing Heart*.

ARTIFICIAL HEART

Q: **Is the artificial heart a real alternative to other forms of heart treatment?**

A: At the moment, no. Any time soon? No.

The quest to find a workable artificial heart has been going on for decades. Different devices using various materials working in individual ways have come and gone. The last such device in the news was the plastic and metal Jarvik 7 artificial heart. What happened in these early operations is that the artificial heart seemed to be doing just the opposite of a bypass: It prolonged life but not its quality. Certainly the recipients no longer gasped for breath or had heart pains, but the first man—Barney Clark— lived a disoriented, hospital-bound life of suffering for 112 days. And William Schroeder, the second recipient, suffered a series of strokes that caused brain damage.

The Jarvik 7 artificial heart is no longer being implanted. The request for approval from the Food and Drug Administration (FDA) was withdrawn in January of 1990 and has not been resubmitted.

Q: Are there any more artificial devices in development?

A: According to the FDA, the newest development is the ventricular assist device, still in the experimental stage. Designed, at least initially, for temporary use to assist a weakened heart, the device is a pump that is externally attached to the heart, although in some cases it may be implanted. The device is powered by an external source—electricity and air—although other designs are testing implantable pumps powered by batteries.

In September of 1991, a Houston man became the first person with a failing heart to recover with a portable, battery-powered heart assist device. (The first recipient died about two weeks after the device was implanted from complications unrelated to the device.) In this second try, the man's diseased heart was left in place, and the mechanical pump—in this case called a left ventricular assist device—is intended to deliver enough oxygenated blood until a heart donor can be found. At the end of 1991, the device had been approved for experimental implant in three more patients.

HEART TRANSPLANT

Q: **How about a heart transplant?**
Is it a workable alternative?

A: Yes and no. Heart transplants work. Since the first human heart transplant on December 3, 1967 —performed by the South African surgeon Christiaan Barnard—hundreds have taken place. A large portion of them died, many too soon after the operation. A good percentage of others have had to have second and even third hearts implanted to keep the person alive. Less than half of those receiving implants live for five years with them. In other words, grasping at the technological straw of heart transplantation in order to stay alive is a 50-50 proposition.

It is no longer the dazzling, news-grabbing event that it used to be, but it is still performed in a few places. There were 1,676 heart transplants performed in the U.S. in 1989.

The problems are many. You have to be a
perfect candidate for a transplant—no other
major underlying illnesses can be afflicting you
because they can get in the way of the procedure.
So if you have a heart in need of replacement
but also have kidney problems or diabetes,
forget it. (In case you wondered—most heart
transplant patients are male, and the average age
is 48 years.)

Let's say you're selected to receive a heart. You
have to wait until the proper donor heart comes
your way. Most people for whom transplantation
is the preferred course of treatment have hearts
so diseased that a wait of a month or so may be
too late. And it is often too late. Hearts don't
grow on trees; they come from donors who
have died or are being kept on life support
machines until the removal surgery can be
performed. Nobody with a heart that suits your
physical needs—blood type, tissue type, other
factors—may turn up all the time you sit and
wait and worry.

Then let's presume you are lucky enough to
get a new heart. There's the problem of rejection
—your body's system fighting off what it
perceives as a threatening, alien body. Your
immune system views this new heart the way it
does bacteria or a virus: something to be
surrounded and escorted out of the body. Plus
there are substances in the donor heart's muscle
tissue or blood supply that may just put up a
death-dealing ruckus when they meet head-on
with your own antibodies and blood factors.
According to the American Heart Association,
9.7 percent of transplant patients die within
30 days.

To fight off rejection, medication is begun
immediately, and the heart recipient will spend

thousands of dollars a month for the rest of his life on anti-rejection medication and other drugs, including drugs that fight the disturbing side effects of the other drugs. Again according to the American Heart Association, the five-year survival rate on a three-drug regimen is almost 81 percent, and the 10-year overall survival rate is over 73 percent. Not bad statistics, *if* you're willing to pay the costs—financial and otherwise.

Many of the same ethical, moral, sociological, and economic (and, perhaps, theological) questions asked of the artificial heart can and must be asked here, especially since not only one but two lives are involved and the concept of what constitutes death is a touchy legal issue. Waiting with $100,000 or more in your hand until someone physically like you dies in a car wreck so that you can live is a strange, psychologically straining method of survival. But for some people, it's the only way out.

CHELATION THERAPY

Q: What exactly is chelation therapy? Is it really a nonsurgical cure for heart disease?

A: To "chelate" means to clamp onto, the way a crab's claws lock around something. In chelation therapy a certain amino acid—ethylenediamine tetraacetic acid (EDTA)—is fed intravenously into the body, with the claim that this substance then chelates the calcium deposits that can be found in clogged arteries. Once EDTA binds with the calcium, so the theory goes, EDTA helps move the calcium out of the artery walls and eventually entirely out of the body itself through excretion by the kidneys. And thus, according to the estimated 1,500 medical professionals who employ EDTA chelation therapy as part or the whole of their practices (many of them are members of the American College of Advancement in Medicine—ACAM), blood is able again to flow freely through the now unobstructed or less-obstructed arteries. Bypass surgery and other invasive procedures can be avoided. Some 300,000 people in the past decade are said to have undergone chelation therapy, many to avoid surgery, others as a last resort when surgery was not possible in their cases.

"Although chelation has been discounted by some physicians, we who do use the therapy are still flabbergasted when we find that 90 percent of a patient's chest pain tends to go away, they can walk farther without leg pains, and vascular problems start improving," says an M.D. in the pages of *Medical Tribune* recently.

Q: **What does the medical establishment think of chelation therapy?**

A: Not much. They have a tough time seeing chelation therapy as anything but very dangerous foolishness and a scientifically unproved concept. They know that chelation therapy has been used for years to remove toxic levels of lead and other heavy metals from the blood-stream. In that regard, it's a long-standing accepted practice. It's just that they don't trust EDTA as an anti-atherosclerotic, they don't believe its alleged benefits, and they don't cotton to the people who profit from it. A regimen of somewhere between 20 and 40 three-gram EDTA infusions, three to four hours each, spread out over eight to 10 weeks on an outpatient basis—a pretty typical treatment pattern—can cost $3,000 to $4,500 or more, not including the slightly expensive preliminary tests. That's certainly cheaper than bypass or balloon angioplasty, but the cost probably will come out of the consumer's pocket. Few insurance companies reimburse for chelation.

Q: **What is it that makes the medical establishment dislike chelation therapy so?**

A: EDTA chelation therapy has worked experimentally in laboratory animals, they concede, but "there is no acceptable evidence that chelation therapy with EDTA is effective in treating human atherosclerosis," concluded the *British Medical Journal* some years back.

At about the same time, statements were made by the American College of Physicians (ACP) and the American Heart Association (AHA)— two organizations not exactly noted for warmly embracing new, maverick therapies—and these statements, surprisingly, didn't come right out and say that EDTA therapy for atherosclerosis was worthless. Rather, the ACP considered chelation therapy "investigational," something that "might possibly be useful, but . . . needs more study in humans before it can be recommended for routine use." The AHA took a similar but harder stand. Its official statement on the matter said, in part: "After reviewing the evidence collected on chelation therapy for atherosclerosis, the American Heart Association concludes that the benefits claimed by this therapy are not scientifically proved [and] recommends that the therapy not be widely applied until it has been rigorously tested in properly controlled clinical trials."

Another thing that really upsets the more established practitioners are the numerous and varied claims of curative powers attributed to EDTA by its supporters, who say EDTA can do everything from saving gangrenous limbs from amputation to reducing or eliminating cancers. It is also said by some to have an anti-aging effect. These sorts of claims infuriate many doctors and scientists and don't help EDTA's credibility in many influential circles, where it is lumped together with laetrile and other "quack" remedies. Anti-EDTA physicians are also upset that by choosing chelation, some patients are delaying "real" treatments for too long.

At best, these doctors think that EDTA chelation therapy works as a **placebo**—a very expensive placebo—and if chelation therapy clinics do anything at all for their patients it's to pay a lot of attention to them, show concern for their ills in a warmer fashion than do most traditional practitioners, and urge on them a healthy exercise and nutrition regimen. And as the *Harvard Medical School Health Newsletter* has grudgingly admitted, "It is conceivable that some of these efforts do contribute to psychological and perhaps physical improvement." But the *Newsletter* adds: "However, there is no reason to think that the chelating agent, EDTA, makes any direct contribution to a person's well-being.''

In short, let it be said that organized medicine has never objected to the use of chelation to remove heavy metals. In that regard, it's a long-standing, accepted practice. Complaints arise when chelation is administered with the claim that EDTA chelates the calcium deposits found in clogged arteries.

Q: How did the idea that EDTA helped athero-sclerosis and heart disease get started?

A: According to one report, a group of doctors in Detroit in the late 1940s gave EDTA to someone or some people who had lead poisoning. As it turned out, they also had atherosclerosis. As the lead poisoning got better, so (claimed the doctors) did the atherosclerosis—the calcium in the artery wall deposits floating away with the toxic heavy metal. Doctors and scientists who don't believe in EDTA's power to do anything but clear metals from the body respond that this thesis is highly questionable, and that the doctor should have run comparative intravenous tests—some with EDTA, some without—instead of what they see as jumping to conclusions.

Q: Is chelation hazardous to your health?
Is that part of the problem?

A: The American Hospital Association, the American College of Physicians, and others have based their hesitation and disapproval partially on EDTA's potential harmful side effects, which include low blood calcium, bone marrow depression, kidney damage, cardiac arrhythmias, convulsions, hypotension, and thrombophlebitis. Furthermore, the deputy director of the National Heart, Lung and Blood Institute was quoted as saying that in most atherosclerosis cases "calcium deposits are an insignificant part of the total lesion. It's predominantly fibrous overgrowth, which would be left behind (in the artery wall) even if the calcium were removed and would be more than enough to cause trouble."

Q: If EDTA is so dangerous, why can't it be banned?

A: EDTA in and of itself, and probably in the three-gram doses given to chelation patients, isn't life threatening unless abused, overprescribed, or sloppily administered. It is not a substance that the FDA can ban, because it has the FDA seal of approval and has had it since 1953—not for heart disease, but for treating heavy metal toxicity. The FDA may disapprove of EDTA's use in this manner, but the substance is okay in their book. Any licensed physician can legally administer EDTA, in any way he or she sees fit or deems valuable.

In turn, lawsuits have been instituted by patients who have been injured by EDTA chelation therapy. Malpractice exists in all walks of medical life, including this one.

Q: What do chelation's supporters say in response to all these charges? How do they defend their therapy?

A: The ACAM doesn't dispute the charges concerning serious toxic and lethal effects of EDTA, but claims they usually occur only when the treatment has been administered incorrectly (as may be the case with standard treatment dispensed by more establishment health professionals). An ACAM spokesman has stated further that the critics in the medical establishment don't really have a very clear picture of what EDTA chelation therapy does in its totality— that the therapy's benefits aren't restricted to locking on to calcium and speeding it out of the body; chelation therapy also increases oxygen utilization and improves the elasticity of the artery walls.

The ACAM has blamed the well-financed medical lobby for blocking research funds for EDTA chelation therapy tests. They have practically begged for the establishment to fund and conduct serious, honest double-blind studies of chelation therapy to help settle the dispute once and for all, but these have not been forthcoming. Most of ACAM's claims are, again, not taken seriously by the orthodoxy because some, if not most, studies are not well done or not in the best scientific tradition. Good news for chelation advocates is that the FDA recently approved a double-blind study of EDTA chelation at three Army hospitals. Double-blind studies are reportedly being conducted at Baylor Medical Center in Houston, and preliminary results from these studies are expected to be out in late 1992.

ACAM also complains that since the patent on EDTA has expired it is in the public domain and thus no pharmaceutical company can make a big financial killing on it, so none of these companies is particularly interested in promoting the substance or its use.

Some chelation advocates say that there are good to excellent results in about 75 percent of patients receiving EDTA, mild improvements in approximately 15 percent, and no improvement in about 10 percent.

Q: **What evidence backs the chelation proponents' claims?**

A: To date, most of the evidence to support EDTA chelation is based on clinical experience rather than clinical trials. There is a distinction: Clinical experience refers to the anecdotal evidence and reports of success compiled by individual doctors as they practice medicine. Clinical trial refers to observations collected by means of comparative tests performed in a laboratory setting. In modern medicine, clinical experience is valuable and often highly persuasive, but clinical trials generally have the final say.

Recent research, while not demonstrating chelation's effectiveness beyond a shadow of a doubt, suggests that chelation merits further clinical investigation. Among this research are small studies reported by H. Richard Casdorph, M.D., Ph.D., in the *Journal of Holistic Medicine*. Casdorph reported a "statistically significant improvement" in blood flow in a group of 18 patients who received EDTA for arteriosclerotic heart disease, and he proposed adding EDTA to the list of calcium-blocking drugs used to open coronary blood vessels.

Another major piece of evidence offered by chelation advocates is a large retrospective analysis of 2,870 patients treated with EDTA. Conducted from May 1983 through September 1985 in Brazil, in accordance with ACAM protocol, the data were published first in the British journal *Medical Hypotheses* in 1988 and republished in the U.S. in the *Journal of Advancement in Medicine* in 1989. According to the results of the analysis, "Eighty-nine percent of all treated patients had marked or good improvement," wrote researchers Efrain Olszewer, M.D., and James P. Carter, M.D., Dr.P.H. Ninety-one percent of the 1,130 patients with peripheral vascular disease (a condition that affects the blood vessels outside the heart and the lymphatic vessels) showed marked improvement—their blood flow returned to normal, and they were able to walk five times farther than before treatment. Seventy-seven percent of patients with ischemic heart disease (a condition caused by blockage of blood flow through the arteries) also showed dramatic improvement.

As for claims that chelation can make improvements beyond those related to heart disease, researchers Olszewer and Carter concluded that EDTA chelation was "of great benefit in the treatment of atherosclerosis."

For the most part, these studies have been criticized by the medical establishment for not being performed as controlled double-blind studies—comparative tests in which one group of patients receives a placebo while another group receives the treatment being tested.

Q: **What can the consumer do who wants to learn more about chelation? Or who wants to discuss the possibility of starting such therapy with a suitable practitioner?**

A: If you decide to explore chelation further, your best bet is to talk with doctors who refuse to administer chelation as well as with doctors who do administer it. Get both sides of the story.

Admittedly, finding a chelation doctor—even to talk with—can be tough. Few physicians advertise chelation therapy services because of the hostility aimed at them by the medical establishment. For assistance, contact ACAM for the names of chelation doctors in your state. (See the section "Informational and Mutual Aid Groups" at the end of this book.)

It's important to remember that chelation therapy is not illegal. EDTA can be prescribed by any licensed M.D. or D.O. You are not breaking the law if you elect to accept it—but you are stepping outside the doors of conventional medical care. If you do so, choose your practitioner with care.

Q: Are chelation doctors all quacks?

A: Not at all. Some are. But, then again, some establishment doctors are, too. Some see a trend—or a fast buck—and pounce. Not all doctors are qualified to administer EDTA chelation, says the American College of Advancement in Medicine. It recommends that you select a doctor who has passed the ACAM's examination and who follows ACAM chelation therapy protocol.

But most of the doctors who use EDTA chelation therapy are sincere, trying to help the ill and frightened, and do it because they see improvements in their patients and believe there is no better, safer, less painful, and less expensive way to treat the people they see. The dispute between doctors on both sides is one of methodology, not reputation; both sides are embarrassed by the quacks and charlatans in their own camps, and want them out.

Q: Is anything new looming on the horizon concerning the nonsurgical treatment of coronary artery disease?

A: Yes, something called coronary atherectomy— known facetiously as "roto-rooter" therapy. Like angioplasty, atherectomy is performed in a cardiac catheterization laboratory. A catheter with a small rotating blade inside a protective cutting chamber is inserted into the patient's groin and advanced until the window in this

chamber is positioned inside the narrowed coronary artery. A hand-held motor is used to inflate a tiny balloon that presses the plaque into the window where the rotating blade shaves it off "like a curl of butter." The debris is pushed into a storage compartment in the catheter tip for safe withdrawal.

Proponents of the procedure tout the minimal hospital stay—usually overnight—following which the patient can quickly resume normal activity. Unfortunately, the design of the new catheter limits its use in all people with coronary artery disease. Best estimates are that 30 percent of patients who qualify for angioplasty can have an atherectomy instead.

4 PREVENTION

Q: Can heart disease be prevented?

A: That is the hope, that is the goal. And in many ways that is the reality. Heredity and sex characteristics aren't changeable aspects of a human life, and catastrophic events like coronary artery spasm or a thromboembolism can occur suddenly and swiftly among even the healthiest of us. But the identification and control of certain factors that increase the risk of heart attack and coronary artery disease may prevent problems in the first place, or may act in a secondary prevention way by averting repeat heart attacks or cleared arteries becoming clogged up again.

SMOKING

Q: **Is it really necessary to go into detail about the hazards of smoking? Doesn't everybody know that it's not good for you?**

A: You'd think so, wouldn't you. But here are two bits of information to mull over:

• The Federal Trade Commission took a survey that included in a true-false section the statement "Cigarette smoking is a major cause of heart disease." Forty percent of all adults and 45 percent of all smokers answered "false" or "don't know."

• A study by the department of psychiatry at the Maryland School of Medicine in Baltimore found that nearly 50 percent of smokers who have heart attacks go right back to smoking within one month of their heart attacks. After six months the percentage is 60 percent. And one of the reasons given was a "disbelief that smoking contributes to heart disease."

So long as people don't know or won't believe that cigarette smoking is a major heart disease risk factor and so long as cigarette companies and their public relations mouthpieces keep sending up expensive smoke screens and double-talk ads and studies performed by people on their payroll—so long as all this continues, it's important to keep plugging and keep reminding that cigarettes are hazardous to your heart's health.

Q: How hazardous is smoking?

A: Extremely. After more than 30 years of research into the subject, the United States Public Health Service has concluded that "cigarette smoking is a major cause of coronary heart disease in the United States for both men and women, and that smoking should be considered the most important of the known modifiable risk factors for CHD [coronary heart disease]." Further, according to the American Heart Association, smokers' risk of heart attack is more than twice that of nonsmokers. In fact, cigarette smoking is the biggest risk factor for sudden cardiac death, and a smoker who has a heart attack is more likely to die from it and more likely to die suddenly (within an hour) than a nonsmoker.

Whew! And as though that's not enough to scare the most hardened and determined of smokers, here are some statistics from the Surgeon General's office to back up the message:

• Cigarette smokers die of CHD at a rate 70 percent greater than nonsmokers.

• The risk of death from smoking increases proportionately to the number of cigarettes you smoke. If you smoke two or more packs a day, your chance of a coronary heart disease death is 200 percent greater than for nonsmokers.

• Smokers "have a two- to fourfold higher risk [of sudden cardiac death] compared to nonsmokers, and the risk appears to be . . . measured by the number of cigarettes smoked per day."

• Cigarette smoking alone is hazardous, but when combined with other risk factors—elevated serum cholesterol and hypertension—the danger is multiplied. Smoking doubles your risk of a

first major coronary event when compared to a
nonsmoker. When high cholesterol is added,
the risk is fourfold, and hypertension makes the
risk eight times as great. Taken another way:
23 out of every 1,000 people have heart
problems with no major risk factors, but have
three risk factors present and that figure is
189 per 1,000. And the risk is even greater if
you have a family history of heart disease.

• '' . . . [It] is estimated that approximately
30 percent of CHD deaths are related to cigarette
smoking, *more* deaths than any other of the
smoking-related diseases, including cancer.''

• More than 300,000 premature deaths in
the U.S. each year are caused by smoking—and
that figure doesn't include such smoking-related
deaths as lung disease and fire.

The Public Health Service sums things up this
way: ''Thus, smoking must be considered the
single most important cause of excess death in
the United States, responsible for almost one of
every six deaths each year in the nation. No other
single, preventable factor in our society exerts a
larger health effect than does cigarette smoking.''

**Q: Do all these smoking statistics apply to
cigars and pipes, too?**

A: It doesn't seem like it. Statistics show that cigar
and pipe smokers are at no increased risk of
coronary heart disease—*unless* they've switched
to them from cigarettes and continue the habit
of inhaling the smoke. If you don't inhale, no
excess risk of heart disease. Tongue or lip
cancer, yes; heart disease, no.

Q: Does it matter how long you've been smoking?

A: It sure does. The three smoking-related elements that bear strongly on development of heart disease are age when you started smoking, how long you've been smoking, and how deeply you inhale.

Q: Even if I've smoked for a long time, will it help me if I quit now?

A: Help you? Your body will positively love you for it. There is a risk reduction almost immediately, and it is absolutely noticeable and significant in a few years after stopping. Here's the key statistic, according to the Public Health Service: "Ten years after cessation [of smoking], the CHD risk of an ex-smoker approaches that of a person who has never smoked."

This also means that you're never too old to quit, a point bolstered by a study at Yale University, which concluded that "smokers older than age 65 years who have been smoking for several decades can benefit from discontinuing smoking."

Statistics from the Framingham Heart Study—the biggest, longest-running heart study in America—showed that men who developed angina before the age of 60 experienced a fourfold reduction in attacks when they gave up smoking.

It's also been found that even if you've had a heart attack already, quitting smoking improves your long-term survival chances.

Q: Are filtered cigarettes safer than nonfiltered ones?

A: Most studies say no. Switching from nonfiltered to filtered cigarettes didn't affect the disease or the death rate, the Framingham Heart Study showed. It might help reduce the cancer rate, but not the CHD rate.

Q: And how about newer brands of cigarettes with low nicotine and carbon monoxide levels?

A: Same story. In the words of researchers at Harvard and Boston Universities, people who smoke those newer types of cigarettes "do not have a lower risk of myocardial infarction than those who smoke cigarettes containing larger amounts of these substances."

Many scientists now believe that carbon monoxide and not nicotine is the real chemical culprit in damaging the cardiovascular system.

Q: How does cigarette smoke cause heart disease and atherosclerosis?

A: It's one of those things where you know it does what it does, but you don't know how it does what you know it does. Researchers at the

Canadian Department of National Health and Welfare put it this way: "The mechanisms by which cigarette smoking might enhance atherogenesis or increase the risk of heart attack have not been satisfactorily established." They add, though, that they doubt there is a "simple, causal relation between cigarette smoking and coronary heart disease," but that there is instead "a complex interaction of toxic effects and constitutional susceptibility." That may explain why some people who smoke multiple packs a day live into old age with few problems.

Q: **Well, if I shouldn't smoke, how about a good chaw? Is chewing tobacco or snuff bad for the heart?**

A: It could be. A study at Texas Lutheran College found that "just a pinch" elevated the heartbeat and blood pressure, not enough to be harmful to healthy folks but sufficiently enough to make it a no-no for people with heart conditions.

Q: **If I don't smoke but everybody around me does, am I at risk of getting heart disease, too?**

A: So-called passive smoking is linked to cancer and pulmonary infections—and certainly to a lot of annoyance and foul-smelling clothes and hair—but the link between this and coronary disease has not been established . . . yet. Right now, nobody knows for sure one way or the other. But what can be said for certain is that "exposure to environmental tobacco smoke cannot be regarded as a safe involuntary habit," in the words of a recent *British Medical Journal* report.

Q: **Women and men seem to be different when it comes to getting heart disease. Are women as affected by smoking as men are?**

A: Without a doubt. Women who smoke, whether they be young or middle-aged, are at an increased risk of having nonfatal heart attacks. A study conducted by the Boston University School of Medicine, the Food and Drug Administration, and the University of Pennsylvania School of Medicine showed that risk of heart attack for women under 50 who smoke is five times greater than for women the same age who don't smoke—and 65 percent of heart attacks among women could be prevented if those women gave up smoking. The danger is greater when other risk factors are involved. Similar findings came out of a Johns Hopkins study.

A combination of cigarette smoking and the taking of oral contraceptives is particularly risky: Women who do both have 10 times higher risk of getting heart attacks than women who do neither.

Q: I'd like to stop smoking, but it's rough. What can I do?

A: It *is* rough. But dying of heart disease is even rougher. Excuse us for getting morbid and melodramatic about it, but every puff is another nail in your coffin, and the sooner you realize that and do something about it, the better.

First of all, you have to want to stop. Second, you may need some help. There are organizations and groups dedicated to getting you to stop. Check these out. They work. They're in the yellow pages, or your local chapter of the American Heart Association (AHA) will tell you how to reach them. Don't throw good money after bad by getting group hypnosis to stop smoking. Successful outcomes of lasting value are rare. Once again, your local AHA chapter might know about this.

Most important of all, though, are the influence and subtle pressure of family and friends. People giving up smoking with loved ones backing them up are more likely to succeed than folks without this support.

HIGH BLOOD PRESSURE

Q: How dangerous is high blood pressure? How does it affect the heart? How is it controlled? Are there nondrug therapies?

A: Good questions, important questions. High blood pressure is such a big topic, you could write a book about it.

And that's precisely what we did. To give this important subject its due would be impossible in the short space we have here. Instead, we refer you to the People's Medical Society book *Blood Pressure: Questions You Have . . . Answers You Need* for the whole story.

Suffice to say, however, that high blood pressure can be a killer. Elevated blood pressure indicates that the heart is working harder than normal, putting both the heart and the arteries under great strain. If high blood pressure isn't treated, the heart may have to work progressively harder to pump enough blood and oxygen to the body's organs and tissues to meet their needs. And when the heart is forced to work harder than normal for an extended time, it tends to enlarge. A slightly enlarged heart may function well, but one that's significantly enlarged has a hard time adequately meeting the demands put on it.

Arteries and **arterioles** also suffer the effects of elevated blood pressure. Over time they become scarred, hardened, and less elastic. This may occur as people age, but elevated blood pressure speeds this process, probably because hypertension accelerates atherosclerosis.

STRESS

Q: **How does stress cause heart disease?**

A: In many ways, not all of them well understood. It can, for example, raise blood pressure high enough to be a problem. It may be a cause of arterial lesions leading to atherosclerotic buildup. It may be an origin of sudden cardiac death (especially after acute emotional shocks or extreme personal crises), coronary artery spasms leading to ischemia, and arrhythmias. Stress releases hormones, some of them not very good for the health of your heart.

Stress is a natural element of human-ness. It's what keeps us alert and bright and, in the misty past, kept us one step ahead of the predators who saw early humanoids as odd-looking cold cuts with legs.

It is today's type of unnatural, work-related stress (*mal*stress, as it is sometimes called) that does the damage. In some studies, so-called Type A personalities—aggressive, ambitious, competitive, workaholic, explosive, trying to cram 18 hours of work into a 12-hour bag—have been identified as prime candidates for heart attacks. Interestingly, the Type A traits are said to be not causes of heart disease but rather symptoms, which, if detected early enough and modified successfully, can put a stop to the coronary risk factor.

A deep sense of loneliness or of being separate from the world also causes a stress that can kill. The bereaved often experience that, and for centuries we've called it dying of a broken heart. Married people have fewer stress-related difficulties than unmarried people do . . . even if the marriage is an unhappy one. There is something about human contact that is of a protective nature.

Q: **How can I reduce or control stress?**

A: You can do everything from changing your life-style to changing your job or getting married—all pretty dramatic therapies. Somewhat more reasonable in the short run is behavior therapy that can help you to relax. Be it biofeedback or meditation or imaging or taking a deep breath and counting to 10 backwards—or going out and giving the ol' one-two to a punching bag at a club or gym—there are ways to reduce stress and save your heart's health. Look into programs sponsored by local health groups or your neighborhood Y.

All this is especially important if you've already had a heart attack. As a British study recently pointed out, heart attack survivors are "significantly more anxious and depressed, significantly more obsessional, and significantly more socially phobic and withdrawn than the general population . . . Such changes . . . may sometimes be amenable to wise counseling."

This was underscored by another study that showed that the rate of second heart attacks among patients who received behavioral therapy fell to 2.8 percent—half the national rate of 6 percent. Behavioral modification, the study concluded, could prevent 15,000 heart attacks a year and save 5,000 lives.

Q: What kind of behavioral modification was that study talking about?

A: Nothing drastic—just sensible. Some basics: no smoking, no big fatty meals, no emotional or physical exhaustion, no caffeine or alcohol to excess, things like that. Plus, no AIAI (aggravation, irritation, anger, impatience) and no stupid triggering mechanism like going crazy over a televised sports event on the weekend. In the study, three repeat heart attacks were directly attributable to TV football games.

There is also more intense, more programmed behavior therapy.

While not every scientist believes in a Type A and Type B categorizing of potential heart attack victims, nearly all still believe that stress and personality traits play a big role in heart disease —and that they can be modified.

EXERCISE

Q: What are the preventive benefits of exercise?

A: The benefits of exercise are widely believed, yet still the subject of some controversy as to effectiveness. What exercise—especially aerobic exercise—seems to be able to do is create a good psychological and emotional atmosphere, release tension and stress, and help you lose some weight.

Exercising the heart and making it stronger can lead to a lower heart rate, a slower pulse. This is good, if it's not *too* slow. Some studies suggest that low heart rate may actually slow down the development of atherosclerosis. Such a strong, enlarged, slow-beating heart is often referred to as "athlete's heart"; it used to be considered a diseased heart but no longer—if the cause of the enlargement is exercise and not something else.

Another important possible result of physical activity of the aerobic type is the development of alternate pathways for oxygenated blood to reach the heart. This theorized collateral system of small arteries can act, in the best of cases, like a natural bypass operation, doing at least part of the job usually relegated to now-blocked major vessels. Norman Cousins believed this was what happened with him.

Exercise can also aid in lowering high blood pressure. Cholesterol levels drop, too (while **high density lipoprotein [HDL]** levels—the so-called good guy cholesterol—rise), but that's probably more because of exercise-related weight loss than properties of exercise itself.

Despite a lack of real hard-core scientific evidence, an exercise program fashioned by a health professional appears to provide huge payoffs.

Q: But can't exercise be dangerous for the heart, too?

A: It sure can. Overdoing it can do you in. Not only that—there's been a fatally false idea circulating that so long as you exercise, you only get healthier and healthier, and atherosclerosis regresses or you become immune to its evils. It's an idea propounded by longtime, true-believer runners and others who can make a profit from such an idea. The idea is that exercise is the ultimate healer. Go tell that to Jim Fixx and the other marathon runners, joggers, and heavy exercisers who have crossed their own personal finish lines before the race was done. Atherosclerosis is usually at the center of sudden cardiac deaths among athletes, and the theory that the running gave suddenly dead runners with heart disease more years than they would have had without the exercise is without any substantiation.

Hard exercising may lead to arrhythmias, although some doctors feel that such heartbeat irregularities in otherwise fit people are not serious.

What seems to be really dangerous is the odd combination of smoking and exercising. Obviously, some people believe that they can neutralize the negative aspects of smoking with the positive values of exercising, especially out in the fresh air. But specifically in men under age 35, this destructive duo may trigger heart attacks.

And isometric exercises for people with heart disease probably should be ruled out. These static, push-and-pull exercises (including weight lifting) tend to raise blood pressure and increase the heart's demand for oxygen, which may in turn bring about a coronary event.

Q:

What sort of exercise program should I involve myself in, especially if I already have a heart condition or have had a heart attack?

A:

Experts in the field recommend this:

• Ask yourself what you would like to do, because you have to like the activity if you're going to make it a lifetime program, which it has to be for it to be successful and effective. Don't pick an activity or exercise that is boring and that you're bound to give up in a few months. It should be a pleasant experience.

• If you think you may grow lax, pick an activity or design a program you can do with someone else. That person will keep you in line . . . and in shape.

• Choose something you can do even if it rains or snows, or have a ready, indoor alternative. Your program has to be a regular one.

• Pick a good time to exercise, one that's easy to set aside every day.

• Start slowly and build up to higher levels. If running is what you want to do, start with brisk walking; then add light jogging. Don't overdo—begin with a program that lasts about a half hour, three times a week.

• Go for aerobic or low-resistance exercises like walking, swimming, running, cycling, and racquet sports. Exercises should use both arms and legs.

• Warm up before exercising and cool down after.

• Avoid exercising in cold weather. It adds stress factors, and breathing cold air can cause the coronary arteries and muscles to tighten up, reducing the flow of oxygen to the heart.

• Don't drink ice cold liquids immediately after exercise. Such a coldness suddenly hitting your system may cause arrhythmia problems. Cool or room temperature liquids are fine.

ALCOHOL

Q: **Alcohol is bad for the heart? I thought I read somewhere that it's *good* for the heart. Who's right?**

A: Both are right. Light to moderate drinking seems to reduce the risk of coronary heart disease. Male moderate drinkers have been found to have as much as a 30 percent lesser chance of having coronary artery disease. What scientists think happens is that the alcohol raises the high density lipoprotein cholesterol, that portion of the total cholesterol picture that's good for your heart health, in a way that somewhat resembles the aftereffects of exercise.

Women as well as men benefit from alcohol's protection. Ex-drinkers, despite years of imbibing, show no such benefit. And since some studies have examined the drinking of beer, others hard liquor, and still others wine, and all arrived at generally the same conclusion, the protector must be alcohol itself, rather than some other substance or chemical in alcohol-containing beverages.

That's the good news. The bad news is that alcohol has no protective effect beyond moderation. To the contrary, it has a destructive effect. Alcohol in not overly large portions can cause what doctors call "holiday heart syndrome": a complex array of arrhythmia disorders. Chronic alcohol consumption can cause cardiomyopathy and conduction disorders. A few drinks downed within an hour negatively affect the muscle fibers of the all-important left ventricle and perhaps cause permanent damage over the long run. And more than modest alcohol use is especially bad for you if you have a preexistent heart condition. Further, excessive alcohol intake (more than two ounces daily) raises blood pressure in some people.

So have a drink now and then, if you wish, unless there is a good health reason not to. Have a glass of wine with dinner, or a nightcap. But only that. And don't binge on weekends or holidays, or you'll pay for it dearly farther along the road.

DIET AND NUTRITION

Q: All you ever hear is cholesterol, cholesterol, cholesterol. What's the big deal about cholesterol anyway?

A: The big deal is that high levels of serum cholesterol—that is, the level of cholesterol in the blood—are implicated in the formation of atherosclerosis and coronary artery disease in nearly every study you can find.

In fact, a very recent examination of data from the Framingham Heart Study has confirmed that high cholesterol levels mean increased risk among people recovering from myocardial infarction. Compared to subjects who had a cholesterol level under 200 mg/dl (within a year after their heart attack), subjects with a cholesterol level over 275 mg/dl had a 3.8 times greater risk of a second heart attack. As reported in the *Annals of Internal Medicine* in late 1991, risk of death from coronary heart disease was found to be 2.6 times greater among the higher-cholesterol subjects. The message from this is loud and clear: If you're recovering from a heart attack, it's critical that you manage your cholesterol level.

Q: Back to the basics—what is cholesterol?

A: A soft, fat-like substance found in all the body's cells, cholesterol is used to form cell membranes, certain hormones, and other necessary substances. Besides being present in human tissues, cholesterol is also found in the bloodstream. The blood transports it to and from various parts of the body. **Hypercholesterolemia** is the term for high levels of cholesterol in the blood.

The liver provides the body with cholesterol in varying amounts, usually about 1,000 mg a day. An additional 400 to 500 mg or more can come directly from foods. Foods from animals—especially egg yolks, meat, fish, poultry, and whole milk products, says the American Heart Association—contain it; foods from plants don't. Typically the body makes all the cholesterol it needs, so it's not something people need to consume to maintain their health.

How cholesterol is involved in forming atherosclerotic plaque isn't perfectly clear. Much of the recent research into cholesterol and lipids (body fats) has focused not so much on total serum cholesterol levels but rather the proportion of HDL to the total cholesterol picture. There is also **low density lipoprotein (LDL)**. What researchers believe about HDL and what causes health writers for popular publications to call it the "good-guy cholesterol" is that HDL escorts excess cholesterol from the body and helps excrete it, while LDL attracts and hangs onto fatty cholesterol and helps deposit it in arteries and cell walls. The way some medical researchers put it is that the problem is not how much cholesterol there is, but how it circulates and what company it keeps—HDL or LDL.

Thus, a high HDL level means less chance of atherosclerosis and heart disease, and a low HDL or high LDL reading indicates trouble ahead. Exercise and moderate alcohol consumption have been shown to increase HDL levels. The higher the HDL level and the lower the total serum cholesterol level, presumably the more protected you are. Some studies have indicated even a regression in plaque when total cholesterol and LDL are lowered and HDL increased.

There is a problem, though.

Q: Of course, there's always a problem. What is it this time?

A: It's that scientists still disagree as to how to lower total cholesterol levels and whether limiting cholesterol in the diet helps to do it to any large degree. They agree that people who already have heart disease ought to be on low-cholesterol diets—why risk the chance?—but that's about all they agree on. It's probably wise and generally healthier to eat a low-fat, low-cholesterol diet, just in case.

Q: How high is high cholesterol?

A: Various doctors have varied levels for alarm, but, conservatively, a reading higher than about 200 milligrams per deciliter of blood will probably raise medical eyebrows and earn you further tests.

Q: Is there such a thing as a cholesterol reading that's too low?

A: Yes. Cholesterol that drops to noteworthy lows sometimes indicates a disease present in the body: perhaps **pernicious anemia** or **hyperthyroidism**.

Also, there is a significant correlation between low cholesterol and cancer, especially colon cancer, but which is the cause and which the effect is a point of some scientific contention.

Q: So what's a good cholesterol level?

A: Again, doctors disagree. Some are on the lenient side and choose numbers that cause their more cautious colleagues to scream. These complainers then promote numbers that others feel strongly are far too low.

Conservatively and safely, under 200 mg/dl—and preferably in the 160 to 180 range—is considered a good level for minimum heart disease risk.

Q: What can I do in terms of diet to reduce my cholesterol level?

A: Even though the jury's still out on the effectiveness of dietary cholesterol reduction in lowering total serum cholesterol—and the role of diet in heart disease altogether—here are some things that might work:

- Eat fewer calories, because losing weight helps. It isn't as important as other risk factors, but it shouldn't be ignored.
- Eat foods rich in fiber.

• Eat more fruits and vegetables, and replace animal fats—especially those that are solid at room temperature—with vegetable oils like corn, safflower, soybean, and sesame. A vegetarian diet may be protective.

• Get yourself a chart of foods and their dietary cholesterol content and place a ceiling of 300 mg a day on your meals.

• Cut down on coffee. One study linked high cholesterol to men who drank three cups a day or more. Besides, caffeine can elevate heart rate and cause arrhythmias that are not of benefit to anybody with heart disease.

Q: **Are there drugs that lower the cholesterol level?**

A: Yes, although as with nearly everything else associated with the study of and research into cholesterol, atherosclerosis, and heart disease, results have been mixed. One of the more recent, more successful experiments saw a drug called cholestyramine reduce serum levels, but under very rigid clinical conditions.

Other drugs used to reduce serum cholesterol levels include colestipol, lovastatin, nicotinic acid, gemfibrozil, and sodium dextrothyroxine.

Only if dietary therapy and weight loss regimen have failed over the course of a year or so should drugs be used. Except in dire emergencies, they should not be the first treatment turned to.

Q: When she isn't talking about cholesterol, my doctor mentions triglycerides. What are triglycerides?

A: Triglycerides are another form of fat in the body, and having a high serum triglyceride reading is as risky as having a high serum cholesterol level. According to the American Heart Association, triglyceride levels normally range from about 50 to 250 mg/dl, depending on age and sex. As people tend to get older (or fatter or both), their triglyceride and cholesterol levels tend to rise. Women also tend to have higher triglyceride levels.

Several clinical studies have shown that an unusually large number of people with coronary heart disease also have high levels of triglycerides in the blood (**hypertriglyceridemia**). However, some people with this problem seem remarkably free from atherosclerosis. Thus, elevated triglycerides, which are often measured along with HDL and LDL, may not directly cause atherosclerosis but may accompany other abnormalities that speed its development.

Q: What about the Pritikin Diet? Isn't it supposed to improve the health of people with heart disease?

A: That's what the Pritikin plan claims, and its proponents have studies to back it up. The program was developed when the late Nathan Pritikin did some research and found that despite the stress and fear experienced by some European peoples during World War II, the incidence of heart disease and heart attacks was very low. Why? Pritikin and others contended that it was the diet: low in fats—milk, cheese, butter, eggs, and meats being difficult to find during the war—and high in fiber and complex carbohydrates. Starting in 1976, Pritikin applied his theories to people who needed help after heart attacks or who wanted to avoid bypass surgery. Many of them who could barely crawl when they arrived at Pritikin's Longevity Centers walked out with the glow of what appeared to be health.

The Pritikin diet is a strict one, limiting daily cholesterol intake to as little as 25 mg. It also prohibits fatty meats (some fish and chicken are allowed), sugar (as well as honey and molasses), salt, eggs, oils, and nuts, among other common staples of the American diet. Fruits and vegetables and whole grains rule the dietary roost. Cholesterol level reductions of 25 percent are claimed by Pritikin people.

Many doctors believe the Pritikin plan is a good one, except for one drawback: It is so inflexible and sometimes so bland that people tend to "fall off the wagon" in search of tasty food. Complete and long-term compliance is all-important in a heart regimen, and if the program itself encourages cheating or noncompliance, it can't be considered *the* answer.

Still, even a modified Pritikin diet would probably do a lot of good for a lot of people, and such food can now be found on restaurant menus and grocery store shelves throughout the U.S. It couldn't hurt to try.

Q: I've heard that eating fish is good for the heart. True?

A: True. It's been known for a long time now—scientific publications have been running studies for years—but ever since the eminent *New England Journal of Medicine* has given it its imprimatur, it's become official: Eating fish even one or two meals a week may significantly reduce the risk of heart attack.

It's the fish oils—rich in eicosapentanoic acid, or omega-3 fatty acid—that do the job, but only the oils of saltwater fish like salmon, tuna, flounder, and cod. The oils appear to reduce triglyceride levels and retard blood platelet aggregation, which in turn may prevent blood clots from forming, getting stuck in atherosclerosis-narrowed coronary arteries, and causing heart attacks.

But fish oil is no miracle drug. Don't expect to be able to eat poorly and smoke, then cancel it out with a tuna fish casserole. Eating fish has to be just one element of a good, overall health program.

Omega-3 fish oils are also available in capsule form.

Q: Is lecithin a heart disease preventive?

A: The dietary supplement lecithin does no good for the heart, and in some instances may do some harm.

Q: What about vitamins and minerals? Any of them good to take for heart disease?

A: Yes. Here's an overview of the most important of them:

Magnesium. It's been shown to aid in keeping blood pressure from becoming high blood pressure. In clinical studies magnesium administered during acute myocardial infarction seemed to reduce the size of the infarct and reduce ventricular abnormalities, too. Magnesium deficiency has been linked to sudden death in patients with ischemic heart diseases, the deficiency causing coronary artery spasm. It's also been implicated in ventricular tachycardia, a heartbeat irregularity, and in chronic heart failure.

A lack of magnesium in the diet and impaired absorption of it, as well as depletion of it due to digitalis toxicity and the use of some diuretics, are all factors in dangerous magnesium deficiency. People who drink "soft" water—stripped of its natural minerals, including magnesium—may be more at risk of heart disease than those who drink "hard" water.

Magnesium supplements (the U.S. recommended daily allowance, or RDA, is 350 milligrams a day for men, 300 milligrams for women) may be useful. Foods high in magnesium include tofu, soy flour, black-eyed peas, wheat germ, nuts (cashews, almonds, brazil nuts, and pecans), peanuts, and kidney and lima beans.

Potassium. Same story here, and it works in concert with magnesium in a balance with calcium and sodium. Potassium depletion leads to arrhythmias; the presence of potassium in healthy amounts is necessary for certain anti-arrhythmia drugs to work properly. There is often a marked potassium deficiency in people who have heart attacks. Potassium deficiency can be caused by the taking of diuretics.

Foods high in potassium include brussels sprouts, cauliflower, avocado, potato, tomato, banana, cantaloupe, peaches, oranges, flounder, salmon, and chicken.

Niacin, once known by the nondescript name of vitamin B-3, is found in a wide variety of foods, such as meat (especially liver), chicken, fish (especially tuna and salmon), whole grains, wheat germ, dairy products, eggs, nuts, dried beans, and peas. It is usually sold as nicotinic acid or, even more commonly, nicotinamide. Niacin's ability to reduce cholesterol levels in the blood has long been recognized, but since it's a vitamin and cannot be patented, no pharmaceutical company has bothered to test and promote it in the fight against heart disease. However, in 1990 researchers from the University of Pennsylvania reported that niacin was the least costly medication available for reducing cholesterol levels—according to their calculations, it can achieve a 1 percent reduction for one-third to one-half the cost of other cholesterol-lowering drugs.

Further, in a collaborative study financed by the National Heart, Lung and Blood Institute, middle-aged men who had already suffered one heart attack and who took large doses of niacin for five years were found to be less likely to have died of a second heart attack. This benefit was seen despite a potentially serious side effect associated with niacin therapy: an increased incidence of abnormal heart rhythms.

Very important to note is the fact that niacin is not without side effects, many of them potentially serious: ranging from flushing, rashes, itching, hives, nausea, diarrhea, and abdominal discomfort to liver malfunction, jaundice, elevated uric acid levels and gout, abnormally high blood sugar levels, peptic ulcers, and the aforementioned abnormal heart rhythms. The soundest advice for anyone is not to self-administer niacin in any form or switch the type already being used without consulting a physician. Further, many experts recommend that people using megadoses of any kind of niacin get liver function tests every few months, as well as periodic checks of blood sugar and uric acid levels.

Selenium and *zinc* are also mentioned frequently as substances that should be found in adequate amounts in the diet (or taken in supplements) to aid in heart health. *Chromium,* too. And *vitamin E* may help raise HDL levels.

Vitamin A—specifically a type of vitamin A called beta carotene—has been shown to promote heart health, too. At the 1991 annual meeting of the American Heart Association, research was presented that showed a 22 percent reduction in heart attack risk with just one serving a day of carrots, spinach, apricots, or other foods rich in beta carotene. Before you stock up with tons of carrots, remember that, as the research team cautioned, the reportedly protective effect of vitamins does not outweigh other heart disease risk factors such as smoking, fatty diets, and high cholesterol levels.

5 OTHER QUESTIONS ABOUT THE HEART AND ITS DISEASES

Q: I'm taking lithium for depression. Is it harmful to the heart?

A: Quite possibly. Lithium has been known to cause heartbeat irregularities and conduction problems. People with heart disease should use lithium salts with extreme caution, if at all. Consult your physician and/or pharmacist.

Q: Is heart disease a geographical problem?

A: Well, incidence of death from heart disease is higher in some places than in others. According to the National Center for Health Statistics, the states with the most heart disease are New Jersey, New York, and Pennsylvania. The Northeast region of the U.S. has the most, followed by the South and then the North Central region. The West has the lowest incidence of heart disease. The state with the lowest is North Dakota, followed by Colorado.

The age of people in these states and regions may be as much a factor as things like stress, hypertension, obesity, sedentary life-style, pollution, economics, and weather.

Q: Is it okay for somebody with heart disease to travel?

A: Usually it's just fine, if you're cautious and prepared for untoward possibilities. A few suggestions, which appeared in the medical journal *Postgraduate Medicine* some years back, are:

• Make use of porter or red cap services where and when you can. Don't feel so chipper and excited that you lose sight of your physical limitations and start hoisting 50-pound wardrobe bags.

• If you are planning to travel by air, consult with your doctor to see if you'll need supplementary oxygen in flight. If so, you'll have to make arrangements with the airline medical department, which should also be informed by you and/or your physician about any other special needs.

• Don't sit in the same position for long periods of time. Once the seat belt signs in the

airplane go off, get up and move around. Same
thing with the train. If traveling in a car, take
breaks. If going by bus, stretch your legs at stops.

• Order a special diet meal—low-cholesterol,
low-salt, vegetarian, etc.—ahead of time if
traveling by air.

• Keep important medications in a bag you
carry with you, especially if traveling by air.
Luggage occasionally gets lost or delayed, and you
can't afford to have that happen to your drugs.

• If you need extra time to get on or off the
plane or train, let somebody with the airline or
Amtrak know ahead of time. They'll make
provisions for you.

Q: **Is there any ethnic group that is more
prone to heart disease than others?**

A: Not many studies look into this subject, but
many of those that do show that Jewish males
are at greater risk than many other ethnic types.
And blacks have an almost one-third greater
chance of having high blood pressure as
compared to whites. Additionally, Puerto Ricans
and Cuban- and Mexican-Americans are more
likely to suffer from high blood pressure than
Anglo-Americans.

Q: Are there work-related hazards that cause or worsen heart disease?

A: Certain occupations expose workers to substances and conditions that may lead to heart disease or to its worsening. Some of the hazards workers may be exposed to are nitrates (leading to angina and heart attack among explosives industry workers), noise, hydrocarbons, and fluorocarbons (causing arrhythmias), among others. Occupational exposure to carbon monoxide, arsenic, lead, and antimony may also cause problems. More study needs to be done in this area.

Q: Is it dangerous to have an operation that has nothing to do with the heart if you have heart disease?

A: An American Heart Association review shows that if you've had a previous heart attack, general surgery and anesthesia will cause a new heart attack in about 6 percent of patients. If the heart attack happened less than three months before surgery, the chance for reinfarction is 30 percent; if the time elapsed is four to six months, the risk drops to 15 percent. Among those who have these surgery-related heart attacks, 50 to 70 percent will die within a week.

In one study of 99 people, there were no cardiac deaths from noncardiac surgery among those who'd had bypass.

People who have had valve replacements seem to be in little danger.

Q: Has heart disease always been America's number one killer?

A: No. Its preeminence as Public Health Enemy Number One is recent, coming as a result of the medical control of other illnesses that were more common.

At the turn of the century, heart disease was fourth among killer conditions. Pneumonia and influenza (that's one category), tuberculosis, and diarrhea and other intestinal ailments were ahead of it.

Slightly more than a decade later, heart disease was on top of the hit parade to stay.

Heart disease is in decline, however—a 34 percent drop between 1983 and 1988, or 124.1 heart disease deaths per 100,000 population in 1988, down from 188.5 per 100,000 in 1983 and 226.4 per 100,000 in 1950. Life-style changes and better, quicker treatment are the usual reasons given for the decline.

Q: When we think of heart disease, more often than not we think of adults. Do children present special problems when it comes to heart disease?

A: The child is father to the adult heart patient. You reap what you sow. The acorn doesn't fall far from the tree.

So much for sappy aphorisms. The point is clear: Nipping heart disease risk factors in the bud early can give your child a chance at a long and heart disease-free life. Here is some information from many studies:

• Dietary, smoking and exercise habits are established early in life. Parents and schools need to be educated about heart disease so that they can influence young children and encourage heart health through example and programs.

Some physicians and researchers believe tests for serum cholesterol levels should begin early in life, at least by school age, and especially among those male children with a family history of heart problems (in fact, children with high cholesterol and triglyceride levels can indicate that their parents, too, have heart disease they may not know about). Some doctors believe infant therapy is more successful than waiting until the child becomes an adolescent or adult. Atherosclerosis may begin with children by the third and fourth grades; if prevented before age 20, it is possible to keep the arteries clean in later life. Tests should also look for diabetes and should keep track of those children who are obese, physically inactive, and have already developed high blood pressure (some do even before kindergarten).

• Early smoking and oral contraceptive use among children and adolescents under age 17 significantly increase cholesterol and triglyceride levels and create a heart disease risk at a young age.

• A hypertensive father can pass on high blood pressure to his children merely through his behavior in coping with anger and stress. In tests, hypertensive fathers' inability to handle situations in the presence of children raised the kids' blood pressure.

• When monkeys were fed a diet simulating that of a typical American child—high in salt and sugar, full of snacks—the poor animals developed high blood pressure. Said one researcher, "Feeding monkeys the diet kids eat is a good model for producing atherosclerosis."

• Surgery to correct pulmonary valve stenosis—a congenital heart disease—can now frequently be done with a balloon-tipped catheter to open the valve pathway, instead of through open-heart surgery. It's a two-day hospital stay, versus as much as two weeks or more for open heart surgery. Ask your surgeon about it.

• Children who need cardiac catheterization run a risk of receiving excessive radiation exposure during the procedure. Parents or guardians ought to be sure that as low a level of radiation as possible is used to observe the catheter move through the artery and that protective shields are in place over sex organs, possibly the eyes, and most important, the thyroid of the exposed child.

Q: Does pregnancy present a danger to women with heart disease?

A: It can, in women with congenital heart defects and valve problems. Late in pregnancy, there may be an increased strain on the heart and lungs that could send the young women into congestive heart failure.

Three things to remember:

• Get lots of information from both the person delivering your baby and a good cardiologist.

• Antibiotics given during labor and delivery may prevent endocarditis and other bacteria-caused damage in women with valvular disorders.

• Don't worry that your child will inherit your congenital defect. It's rare when that happens.

INFORMATIONAL
AND
MUTUAL AID GROUPS

American College of Advancement in Medicine

23121 Verdugo Drive, Suite 204
Laguna Hills, CA 92653
714-583-7666

American Heart Association

7272 Greenville Avenue
Dallas, TX 75231
214-373-6300

Coronary Club, Inc.

9500 Euclid Avenue
Cleveland, OH 44195
216-444-3690

Mended Hearts

7320 Greenville Avenue
Dallas, TX 75231
214-706-1442

National Heart, Lung and Blood Institute

120/80 National Institutes
of Health
Bethesda, MD 20208
301-951-3260

GLOSSARY

Acute nonspecific pericarditis: A condition in which the pericarditis is not secondary to another disease, but rather is attacked directly itself by a virus. See also **Pericarditis**.

Acute pericarditis: See **Pericarditis**.

Anemia: A condition in which the blood is deficient in red blood cells, in hemoglobin, or in total volume.

Angina pectoris: Medical term for a severe, suffocating chest pain caused by an insufficient amount of blood being supplied to the heart muscle.

Angiography: An imaging procedure that enables blood vessels to be seen on film after the vessels have been filled with a contrast medium, which is a substance that is opaque to X rays. It is used to detect diseases that alter the appearance of the blood vessel channel.

Annuloplasty: A kind of plastic surgery in which heart valve tissue is reconstructed.

Aorta: The body's primary artery that receives blood from the heart's left ventricle and distributes it to the body.

Aortic stenosis: An obstruction to the flow of blood from the left ventricle to the aorta.

Aortic valve: The heart valve between the left ventricle and the aorta. It has three flaps, or cusps.

Arrhythmia (or Dysrhythmia): An abnormal rhythm of the heart.

Arteriole: A small branch of an artery that links the artery to a capillary.

Arteriosclerosis: Commonly known as "hardening of the arteries." A degenerative condition caused by accumulation of minerals and fatty deposits in the arteries, causing a rigidity and inflexibility that affects the flow of blood through the body.

Artery: A blood vessel that carries blood away from the heart.

Atheroma: A fatty mass, covered by fibrous substance, and existing as a plaque in an artery wall.

Atherosclerosis: The most prevalent form of arteriosclerosis in which the inner layers of artery walls become thick and irregular due to deposits of fat, cholesterol, and other substances. As the interior walls of arteries become lined with layers of these deposits, the arteries become narrowed, and the flow of blood through them is reduced.

Atrial fibrillation: A type of irregular heartbeat in which the upper chambers of the heart beat irregularly and very rapidly.

Atrial flutter: A type of irregular heartbeat in which the upper chambers of the heart beat very rapidly.

Atrial paroxysmal tachycardia: A condition in which the heartbeat suddenly becomes abnormally fast—with beats of up to 220 a minute—then just as suddenly returns to normal.

Atrioventricular (AV) node: A small mass of specialized conducting tissue at the bottom of the right atrium through which the electrical impulse stimulating the heart to contract must pass to reach the ventricles.

Atrium: Either one of two upper chambers of the heart in which blood collects before being passed to the ventricles; also called auricle.

Beta blocker: A drug principally used to treat heart disorders such as high blood pressure, angina pectoris, and cardiac arrhythmia.

Bilateral oophorectomy: Removal of both ovaries.

Bradycardia: An abnormally slow heartbeat.

Calcium channel blocker: A drug used to treat angina pectoris, high blood pressure, and certain types of cardiac arrhythmias.

Capillary: Any of the minute vessels that carry blood between the smallest arteries and the smallest veins.

Cardiac catheterization: The process wherein a thin, flexible tube is inserted in a locally anesthetized patient, and then pushed along through a blood vessel (usually in the groin or arm areas) and on into the heart, for the purpose of examination.

Cardiac tamponade: Compression of the heart.

Cardiomyopathy: A serious disease involving an inflammation and decreased function in heart muscle.

Cardiopulmonary resuscitation (CPR): A technique combining chest compression and mouth-to-mouth breathing; used during cardiac arrest to keep oxygenated blood flowing to the heart muscle and brain until advanced life support can be started.

CAT scan or Computerized tomography scanning: A computer-enhanced series of cross-sectional X-ray images of a selected part of the body. This test can detect many conditions that cannot be seen in regular X rays.

Commissurotomy: A procedure in which heart valve leaflets—stuck together because of the scar tissue formed after a bout with rheumatic-fever-induced endocarditis—are separated.

Congenital: Denotes conditions existing at birth.

Congestive heart failure: A group of conditions involving a weak and failing heart and congestion, usually in the lungs.

Constrictive pericarditis: A condition in which the pericardium becomes scarred and hard and full of calcium deposits. The heart is no longer free to move about, and its duties are interfered with.

Coronary arteries: Two arteries arising from the aorta that arch down over the top of the heart, branch out, and provide blood to the heart muscle.

Defibrillation: Electric shocks delivered to the heart.

Defibrillator: An electronic device—basically two metal paddles connected to a source of high-voltage electricity—that helps reestablish normal contraction rhythms in a malfunctioning heart.

Dextroposition of the aorta: A defect in which the aorta gets blood from both the right and left ventricles.

Diastole: The lowest blood pressure measured in the arteries. It occurs when the heart is at rest, between heartbeats.

Digitalis (also Digoxin, Digitoxin): A drug that strengthens the contraction of the heart muscle, slows the rate of contraction of the heart, and promotes the elimination of fluid from body tissues.

Dilatation: A condition in which a cavity, tube, or opening is enlarged or stretched; may result from normal physiological process or from disease (as in the case of the heart).

Diuretic: A drug that promotes urination, thus speeding the elimination of sodium and water. This is an effective and much-prescribed method of blood pressure control.

Echocardiography: A diagnostic technique in which pulses of sound are transmitted into the body and the echoes returning from the surfaces of the heart and other structures are electronically recorded.

Electrocardiogram (EKG or ECG): A graphic record of electrical impulses produced by the heart.

Endocarditis: An inflammation of the internal lining of the heart, particularly the valves, because of an infection.

Endocardium: The internal lining of the heart.

False-negative result: Test shows up negative, or normal, but disease is actually present.

False-positive result: Test shows up positive, or abnormal, but no disease is actually present.

Fluoroscopy: A specialized X-ray procedure. It provides moving images of the body at work, in order to show abnormalities in size, shape, position, or functioning of various parts of the body.

Heart block: A disorder of the heartbeat that may lead to dizziness, fainting, attacks, or strokes; caused by an interruption to the passage of impulses through the specialized conducting system of the heart.

Hemoglobin: The oxygen-carrying pigment found in red blood cells.

High blood pressure: See **Hypertension**.

High density lipoprotein (HDL): A carrier of cholesterol believed to transport cholesterol away from the tissues and to the liver, where it can be excreted.

Hypercholesterolemia: A high level of cholesterol in the blood.

Hypertension: A chronic increase in blood pressure above its normal range.

Hyperthyroidism: A condition in which the thyroid gland functions excessively. Goiter is a common physical sign of hyperthyroidism.

Hypertriglyceridemia: A high level of triglycerides in the blood.

Hypertrophy: Enlargement of an organ or tissue.

Hypotension: Low blood pressure. A person is usually considered hypotensive if he or she has continual blood pressure readings in which the systolic reading is less than 100 mm/Hg.

Hypothermia: A fall in body temperature to below 95 °F (35 °C).

Hypothyroidism: Deficient activity of the thyroid gland resulting in under-production of thyroid hormones.

Hypoxia: An inadequate amount of oxygen to the tissues.

Infarction: Death of an area of tissue caused by lack of blood supply.

Inferior vena cava: One of two very large veins into which all the circulating deoxygenated blood drains; starts in the lower abdomen and travels some 10 inches upward before connecting to the right atrium. It collects blood from all parts of the body below the chest.

Ischemia: Decreased blood flow to an organ, usually due to obstruction of an artery.

Laser coronary angioplasty: A procedure for treating a narrowing or blockage of a blood vessel. A catheter one-eighth of an inch in diameter is inserted into the vessel and pushed forward to the coronary occlusion. At that point, instead of inflating a balloon (as in balloon angioplasty), the doctor in charge aims an argon laser beam at the fatty deposits clogging the blood path and disintegrates the blockage.

Left atrium: See **Atrium**.

Left ventricle: See **Ventricle**.

Low blood pressure: See **Hypotension**.

Low density lipoprotein (LDL): The main carrier of harmful cholesterol in the blood.

Magnetic resonance imaging (MRI): A diagnostic technique that provides high-quality cross-sectional images of organs and structures within the body without radiation; produces especially detailed images of the heart, major blood vessels, and blood flow.

Mediastinum: The space between the lungs and the structures within that space. It contains the heart, windpipe, esophagus, the major blood vessels entering and leaving the heart, lymph nodes and lymphatic vessels, thymus gland, and various nerves.

Mitral valve: The heart valve between the left atrium and left ventricle. It has two flaps, or cusps.

Myocardial infarction (MI): The damaging or death of an area of the heart muscle resulting from a reduced blood supply to that area; a heart attack.

Myocardium: The muscular wall of the heart. It contracts to pump blood out of the heart and then relaxes as the heart fills with returning blood.

Necrotic: Pertaining to or characterized by death of tissue.

Occlusion: Blockage of any passage, canal, vessel, or opening in the body.

Percutaneous transluminal coronary angioplasty (PTCA) (or Balloon Angioplasty): A procedure for treating a narrowing or blockage of a blood vessel or heart valve. A catheter with a deflated balloon on its tip is passed into the narrowed artery segment, the balloon inflated, and the narrowed segment widened.

Pericardial effusion: A condition in which the pericardium becomes somewhat flooded with liquid. The liquid, or effusion, comes either from outside the pericardium or from the pericardium itself due to injury.

Pericardiocentesis: Drainage of excess of fluid (effusion) from within the pericardium; sometimes called a pericardial tap.

Pericarditis: Inflammation of the pericardium, the outer membrane surrounding the heart, leading in many cases to chest pain and fever.

Pericardium: The outer sac that surrounds the heart.

Pernicious anemia: A type of anemia caused by vitamin B12 deficiency.

Placebo: An chemically inert or innocuous substance given in place of a drug.

Plaque: A deposit of fatty (and other) substances in the inner lining of the artery wall characteristic of atherosclerosis.

Pleurisy: Inflammation of the membrane lining the lungs and chest cavity (pleura).

Pulmonary artery: The blood vessel that carries blood from the heart to the lungs.

Pulmonary edema: Fluid retention in the lungs.

Pulmonic, or Pulmonary, valve: The heart valve between the right ventricle and the pulmonary artery. It has three flaps, or cusps.

Rheumatic fever: A disease that causes inflammation in various tissues throughout the body. The main serious effect on the heart can be a thickening or scarring of the heart's valves, leading to narrowing and/or leaking of the valves.

Right atrium: See **Atrium**.

Right ventricle: See **Ventricle**.

Right ventricular hypertrophy: An increase of volume of the myocardium of the right ventricle.

Sclerosis: A hardening of tissue.

Sick sinus-node syndrome: Abnormal function of the heart's natural pacemaker that leads to a slow heart rate.

Sinus bradycardia: A slow, regular heart rate caused by reduced electrical activity in the heart's natural pacemaker.

Sinus, or sinoatrial (S-A), node: The heart's natural pacemaker, which produces the electrical impulses that travel down to eventually reach the ventricular muscle, causing the heart to contract.

Sphygmomanometer: An instrument for measuring blood pressure.

Sternum: The breastbone.

Stethoscope: An instrument for listening to sounds within the body.

Streptokinase: A drug used to dissolve blood clots. Given in the early stages of a heart attack, it may limit the damage caused to the heart muscle.

Stress test: An exercise or stress electrocardiogram which evaluates the heart's response to the stress of physical exercise; most often performed to determine the cause of unexplained chest pain when coronary heart disease is suspected.

Superior vena cava: One of two very large veins into which all the circulating deoxygenated blood drains; starts at the top of the chest and travels some three inches downward before connecting to the right atrium. It collects blood from the upper trunk, head, neck, and limbs.

Syncope: Fainting, as a result of insufficient blood flow to the brain.

Systole: The highest blood pressure measured in the arteries. It occurs when the heart contracts with each heartbeat.

Tachycardia: A dangerous, abnormally fast heartbeat.

Thromboembolism: The blockage of a blood vessel by a particle that has broken away from a blood clot.

Thrombosis: The formation or presence of a blood clot inside a blood vessel or cavity of the heart.

Thrombus: A blood clot that forms inside a blood vessel or cavity of the heart.

Tissue-type plasminogen activator (TPA): A genetically engineered enzyme that dissolves blood clots. It is used in the treatment of heart attack, severe progressive angina pectoris, and blockage of an artery.

Tricuspid valve: The heart valve between the right atrium and the right ventricle. It has three flaps, or cusps.

Triglyceride: A fat that comes from food or is made in the body from other energy sources such as carbohydrates.

Valvular regurgitation: A backflow of liquid from valves.

Vasodilator: A drug that causes the muscle in the walls of blood vessels (especially arteries) to relax, allowing the artery to dilate, or widen.

Vein: A blood vessel that returns blood toward the heart from the various organs and tissues of the body.

Ventricle: One of the two lower chambers of the heart.

Ventricular aneurysm: A ballooning of a portion of the wall of the left ventricle due to the pressure of blood flowing through a weakened area.

Ventricular fibrillation: A condition in which the ventricles contract in such a rapid, nonsynchronous, uncoordinated fashion that no blood is pumped from the heart; often happens early in a heart attack.

SUGGESTED READING

Braunwald, Eugene. *Heart Disease: A Textbook of Cardiovascular Medicine.* 3d ed. Philadelphia: W. B. Saunders, 1988.

Budnick, Herbert N., and Scott Robert Hays. *Heart to Heart: A Guide to the Psychological Aspects of Heart Disease.* Santa Fe, NM: Health Press, 1991.

Charash, Bruce D. *Heart Myths.* New York: Viking, 1991.

Cooper, Kenneth. *Controlling Cholesterol: Preventive Medicine Program.* New York: Bantam, 1989.

Dorland's Illustrated Medical Dictionary. 27th ed. Philadelphia: W. B. Saunders, 1988.

Dranov, Paula. *Heart Disease: A Random House Personal Medical Handbook.* New York: Random House, 1990.

Eshleman, Ruthe, and Mary Winston. *American Heart Association Cookbook.* 5th ed. New York: Times Books, 1991.

Frohlich, Edward D., and Genell J. Subak-Sharpe. *Take Heart: Cut Your Inherited Risks of Heart Disease.* New York: Crown, 1990.

Gordon, Neil F., and Larry W. Gibbons. *The Cooper Clinic Cardiac Rehabilitation Program.* New York: Simon & Schuster, 1990.

Hellerstein, Herman, and Paul Perry. *Healing Your Heart: A Proven Program for Lowering Cholesterol and Preventing or Healing Heart Disease.* New York: Simon & Schuster, 1990.

Horovitz, Emmanuel. *Cholesterol Control Made Easy: How to Lower Your Cholesterol for a Healthier Heart.* Encino, CA: Health Trend, 1990.

Karpman, Harold L. *Preventing Silent Heart Disease: Detecting and Preventing America's Number 1 Killer.* New York: Crown, 1989.

Khan, M. Gabriel. *Heart Attacks, Hypertension, and Heart Drugs.* Emmaus, PA: Rodale, 1986.

Klieman, Charles, and Kevin Osborn. *If It Runs in Your Family: Heart Disease: Reducing Your Risk.* New York: Bantam, 1991.

Kowalski, Robert E. *The 8-Week Cholesterol Cure: How to Lower Your Blood Cholesterol by up to 40 Percent without Drugs or Deprivation.* New York: Harper & Row, 1987.

Kowalski, Robert E. *8 Steps to a Healthy Heart: The Complete Guide to Heart Disease Prevention and Recovery from Heart Attack and Bypass Surgery.* New York: Warner Books, 1992.

Larson, David E., M.D., et al., eds. "The Heart and Blood Vessels." In *The Mayo Clinic Family Health Book.* New York: Morrow, 1990.

Oexmann, Mary Joan. *The Heart Factor Food Plan.* New York: Morrow, 1990.

Ornish, Dean, M.D. *Dr. Dean Ornish's Program for Reversing Heart Disease.* New York: Random House, 1990.

Pantano, James A. *Living with Angina.* New York: Harper & Row, 1990.

Rejuvenate Your Heart: Over 40 Tips to Protect Your Heart. Emmaus, PA: Rodale, 1990.

Rothfeder, Jeffery. *Heart Rhythms: Breakthrough Treatments for Cardiac Arrhythmia—the Silent Killer of 400,000 Americans Each Year.* Boston: Little, Brown, 1989.

Samuels, Mike, and Nancy Samuels. *Heart Disease: How to Work with Your Doctor and Take Charge of Your Health.* New York: Summit Books, 1991.

Schlant, Robert C. *The Heart: Arteries and Veins.* 7th ed. New York: McGraw-Hill, 1990.

Schoenberg, Jane, and JoAnn Stichman. *Heart Family Handbook: A Complete Guide for the Entire Family of Anyone with any Heart Condition.* Philadelphia: Hanley & Belfus, 1990.

INDEX

A

ACAM. *See* American College of Advancement in Medicine (ACAM)

ACE. *See* Angiotensin converting enzyme (ACE) inhibitors

Acute nonspecific pericarditis. *See* Pericarditis, acute nonspecific

Acute pericarditis. *See* Pericarditis, acute

Adolescents. *See* Children

AEM devices. *See* Ambulatory electrocardiographic monitoring (AEM) devices

Age
   angioplasty and, 90
   bypass surgery and, 89-91

Airports, heart disease and, 21

Alcohol
   arrhythmias and, 144
   cardiomyopathy and, 53, 144
   congenital heart defects and, 31
   heart disease and, 19, 73, 143-44

Allergic reactions, cardiac deaths and, 21-22

Ambulatory electrocardiographic monitoring (AEM) devices, 14

American College of Advancement in Medicine (ACAM), 164, chelation therapy and, 116, 121-25

Anemia, 165
   pernicious, 171
      cholesterol and, 147

Angina pectoris, 165
   angioplasty, laser coronary, 108-9
   bypass surgery and, 61, 90-91, 94, 96, 99, 101-2, 104
   cardiomyopathy and, 53
   causes of, 57-58
   congestive heart failure and, 25
   coronary artery disease and, 86
   diagnosis of, 59
   medication therapy and, 101-2
   myocardial infarction and, 58, 63, 66, 101-2
   nitrates and, 159
   smoking and, 131
   treatment for, 58, 60-61, 167, 172

Angiocardiography, 16

Angiography, 15, 165
   angina and, 59
   bypass surgery and, 94
   valvular heart disease and, 36-37

Angioplasty, 170
   laser coronary, 70, 71, 170
      angina and, 108-9
      atherosclerosis and, 108-9
      bypass vs., 100
      percutaneous transluminal coronary angioplasty (PTCA) vs., 108-9, 170
      safety of, 109
   percutaneous transluminal coronary (PTCA), 103
      age and, 90
      bypass surgery vs., 95, 100, 102-8
      complications with, 104-8
      coronary artery disease and, 102-8
      coronary atherectomy and, 126
      costs of, 104, 117
      ischemia and, 103
      mortality and, 105
      myocardial infarction and, 106
      preventive, 106
      recovery after, 104
      restenosis and, 105-6
      self help vs., 110-11
      streptokinase and, 103

Angiotensin converting enzyme (ACE) inhibitors, congestive heart failure and, 29-30

Annuloplasty, 37, 165, valvular heart disease and, 37, 165

Antibiotics
   pericarditis, acute and, 55
   pregnancy with heart disease and, 163
   surgery, valve replacement and, 39

Anticoagulants, side effects of, 39

Antimony, heart disease and, 159

Aorta, 5, 165

Aortic stenosis. *See* Stenosis, aortic

Arrhythmia, 14, 23, 40-51, 166
   alcohol and, 144
   atrial fibrillation, 42, 166
   atrial flutter, 42, 166
   atrial paroxysmal tachycardia, 42, 166
   beta blockers and, 167
   caffeine and, 149
   causes of, 40-41, 137, 143
   congestive heart failure and, 26
   exercise and, 141
   fluorocarbons and, 159
   heart block, 42, 47, 169
   myocardial infarction and, 67
   potassium and, 153-54
   sinus bradycardia, 41-42, 47, 171
   sick sinus node syndrome, 42, 47, 171
   stress and, 137
   treatment for, 42-51, 167
   ventricular fibrillation, 42-43, 72, 173

Arsenic, heart disease and, 159

Arteries, 166
aorta, 5, 165
coronary, 6, 168
pulmonary, 5, 171

Arterioles, 166, hypertension and, 136

Arteriosclerosis, 166

Artificial devices
artificial heart, 111-12
ventricular assist device, 112

Artificial heart, 111-12

Aspirin, myocardial infarction and, 79-81

Atheroma, 86, 166. *See also* Plaque

Atherosclerosis, 20, 166
angina and, 57
angioplasty, laser coronary and, 108-9, 170
bypass surgery and, 94-97
chelation therapy and, 115-20, 123-24
children and, 161
cholesterol and, 144, 146
coronary artery disease and, 86
exercise and, 140-41
fish oil and, 152
hypertension and, 136
sickle cell anemia and, 20
smoking and, 132-33
triglycerides and, 150

Atrial fibrillation, 42, 166

Atrial flutter, 42, 166

Atrial paroxysmal tachycardia. *See* Tachycardia, atrial paroxysmal

Atrial septal defect, 34

Atrium, 4-5, 166

B

Balloon angioplasty. *See* Angioplasty, percutaneous transluminal coronary (PTCA)

Behavior therapy, stress and, 138-39

Beta blockers, 167
angina and, 102, 167
myocardial infarction and, 83-84

Beta carotene, heart disease and, 155

Bibliography, 174-75

Bilateral oophorectomy, 167, myocardial infarction and, 81

Blood clot. *See* Thromboembolism, Thrombosis, Thrombus

Blood flow
angina and, 57-58
heart function and, 5-6

Blood pressure, 10-11
See also Hypertension, Hypotension
angina and, 60
vasodilators and, 21

Blood-thinners. *See* Anticoagulants

Blue babies. *See* Tetralogy of Fallot

Body fats. *See* Cholesterol

Bradycardia, 40, 167
arrhythmias and, 40
sinus, 41-42, 47, 171

Breastbone. *See* Sternum

Breathing difficulties, cardiomyopathy and, 53

Bypass surgery, 88-111
age and, 89-91
angina and, 61, 90-91, 94, 96, 99, 101-2, 104
angiography and, 94
alternatives to, 95, 100-26
cardiac catheterization and, 95, 98
costs of, 87, 97-99, 101, 104, 117
diet and, 96
gender and, 91
health insurance and, 98-99
incidence of, 87, 91, 99-100
mortality and, 90-91
myocardial infarction after, 99, 101
prognosis after, 95-97
race and, 99-100
reasons for, 94-95
side effects of, 92
smoking and, 96
surgery, noncardiac and, 159
valve replacement surgery and, 39
women and, 91

C

Caffeine, arrhythmias and, 149

Calcium channel blockers, 60-61, 83, 102, 167
angina and, 60-61, 102
myocardial infarction and, 83
diltiazem, 60
nifedipine, 60
side effects of, 60
verapimil, 60

Calcium deposits, chelation therapy and, 115-16, 119-21, 123

Cancer
See also Chemotherapy
cholesterol and, 148
hormones and, 77
pericardial effusion and, 55
smoking and, 130, 132-33

Capillaries, 167

Captopril, 28

Carbon monoxide
heart disease and, 159
smoking and, 132

Carbon tetrachloride, cardiomyopathy and, 53

Cardiac arrest, 22, 44, 46, 72

Cardiac catheterization, 15-17, 167
   bypass surgery and, 95, 98
   children and, 162
   fluoroscopy and, 16
   incidence of, 98
   murmurs and, 32-33
   overuse of, 17
   valvular heart disease and, 36-37

Cardiac tamponade, 56, 167

Cardiomyopathy, 167
   alcohol and, 144
   angina pectoris and, 53
   cardiac output and, 52
   congestive heart failure and, 52-54
   etiology of, 52-53
   symptoms of, 53
   treatment for, 53-54
   valvular regurgitation and, 52

Cardiopulmonary resuscitation (CPR), 167
   arrhythmias and, 43-44
   myocardial infarction and, 66

CAT scans. See Computerized tomography scans

Chelation therapy, 115-25
   American College of Advancement in
      Medicine (ACAM) and, 116, 121-25
   atherosclerosis and, 115-20, 123-24
   bypass surgery vs., 116
   calcium deposits and, 115-16, 119-21, 123
   costs of, 117
   ethylenediamine tetraacetic acid (EDTA)
      and, 115-25
   Food and Drug Administration (FDA)
      and, 120-22
   lead and, 116, 119
   medical establishment views on, 116-20
   practitioners of, 124-25
   side effects of, 120

Chemical exposure, myocardial infarction
   and toxic, 85

Chemotherapy, cardiomyopathy and, 53

Chest pain. See Angina pectoris,
   Myocardial infarction

Children
   atherosclerosis and, 161
   cardiac catheterization and, 162
   diet of American, 161-62
   heart disease and, 160-62
   hypertension and, 161-62
   open heart surgery and, 162
   radiation and, 162

Cholesterol
   See also Triglycerides
   anemia, pernicious and, 147
   atherosclerosis and, 144, 146
   cancer and, 148
   coronary artery disease and, 144
   diet and, 144-55
   exercise and, 140
   Framingham Heart Study and, 144-45
   heart disease and, 19, 86, 144-55, 161
   high density lipoprotein (HDL), 140, 146,
      150, 169
   hyperthyroidism and, 147

   low density lipoprotein (LDL), 146, 150, 170
   medication therapy for reduction of, 149
   myocardial infarction and, 75, 144-45
   plaque and, 146
   reduction of, 148-49
   smoking and, 129-30
   sources of, 145

Cholestyramine, cholesterol reduction with, 149

Chronic heart failure, magnesium and, 153

Clot busting drugs, 68-69
   Eminase, 69
   side effects of, 69
   streptokinase, 68-69, 71
   tissue-type plasminogen activator (T.P.A.),
      69, 84

Clot. See Thromboembolism, Thrombosis,
   Thrombus

Coarctation of the aorta, 35

Coffee, arrhythmias and, 149

Colestipol, cholesterol reduction with, 149

Commissurotomy, valvular heart disease and,
   37, 167

Compensatory mechanisms, congestive heart
   failure and, 25-26

Computerized tomography scans, 167,
   murmurs and, 33

Congenital heart defects
   See also Congenital, 167
   atrial septal defect, 34
   coarctation of the aorta, 35
   dextroposition of the aorta, 34
   diagnosis of, 31-33
   etiology of, 30-32
   incidence of, 30, 163
   murmurs and, 32-33
   patent ductus arteriosus, 34
   pregnancy with heart disease and, 162-63
   prognosis with, 31
   pulmonary stenosis, 33-34, 162
   surgery and, 31-34
   tetralogy of Fallot, 33-34
   ventricular hypertrophy, 34
   ventricular septal defect, 33-34

Congestive heart failure, 167
   angina pectoris and, 25
   cardiomyopathy and, 52-54
   causes of, 24
   myocardial infarction and, 70
   physiology of, 23
   pregnancy and, 162
   propranolol and, 44
   symptoms of, 24
   treatment for, 27-30

Constrictive pericarditis, 56, 167

Contraceptives, oral
   children and, 161
   myocardial infarction and, 81-82, 134
   smoking and, 134

Coronary arteriography, 16

Coronary artery bypass grafting.
  See Bypass surgery

Coronary artery disease
  ambulatory electrocardiographic monitoring
    (AEM) device and, 14
  angina pectoris and, 86
  angioplasty and, 102-8
  atherosclerosis and, 86
  bypass surgery and, 96
  cardiac catheterization and, 16
  cholesterol and, 144
  coronary atherectomy and, 125-26
  costs of, 87
  incidence of, 87
  manifestations of, 86-87
  mortality and, 87
  risk factors for, 86, 127
  sex differences in management of, 64
  treatment for, 87-126
  valvular heart disease and, 39

Coronary artery spasm, 127
  angina and, 57
  magnesium and, 153
  stress and, 137

Coronary Artery Surgery Study (CASS), 100-2

Coronary atherectomy
  angioplasty and, 126
  coronary artery disease and, 125-26

Coronary spasm, 83

Cortisone, acute pericarditis and, 55

Cousins, Norman, myocardial infarction
  self help and, 110-11, 140

CPR. *See* Cardiopulmonary resuscitation (CPR)

Cyanosis, 34

D

Defibrillation, 168, arrhythmias and, 45-46

Defibrillator, 168

Dextroposition of the aorta, 34, 168

Diabetes
  coronary artery disease and, 86
  myocardial infarction and, 73

Diagnosis-related groups (DRGs), pacemakers
  and Medicare's, 51

Diarrhea, mortality and, 160

Diastole, 10, 168

Diet
  American children and, 161-62
  cholesterol, 144-55
  congestive heart failure and, 27
  heart disease and, 20, 96, 144-55, 161
  myocardial infarction and, 78
  Pritikin Diet, 150-51

Digitalis, 168
  angina and, 60
  arrhythmias and, 41
  congestive heart failure and, 28
  magnesium and, 153
  side effects of, 28-29
  treatment for toxicity with, 43

Digitoxin. *See* Digitalis

Digoxin. *See* Digitalis

Dilatation, 26, 168, congestive heart failure
  and, 26

Diuretics
  angina and, 60
  congestive heart failure and, 28-29

Down's syndrome, congenital heart defects
  and, 31

DRGs. *See* Diagnosis-related groups (DRGs)

Dysrhythmia. *See* Arrhythmia

E

ECG. *See* Electrocardiogram

Echocardiography, 15, 168
  murmurs and, 33
  valvular heart disease and, 36

Edema, pulmonary, 24-25, 171

EDTA. *See* Ethylenediamine tetraacetic
  acid (EDTA)

Eicosapentanoic acid, 152

Eisenmenger's syndrome, 34

EKG. *See* Electrocardiogram

Electrical stimulation, arrhythmias and, 43-51.
  See also Defibrillation, Pacemakers

Electrocardiogram, 12-15, 168
  angina and, 59
  murmurs and, 32
  myocardial infarction and, 63, 65

Eminase, myocardial infarction and, 69

Enalapril, congestive heart failure and, 29-30

Endocarditis, 35-36, 168, valve replacement
  surgery and, 39

Endocardium, 7, 168

Enzymes, myocardial infarction and,
  63, 68-69, 84

Estradiol. *See* Estrogen

Estrogen, myocardial infarction and,
  20-21, 76-77

Ethnic groups
  heart disease and, 158
  hypertension and, 158

Ethylenediamine tetraacetic acid (EDTA),
  chelation therapy and, 115-25

Exercise
    aerobic, 139
    arrhythmias and, 141
    atherosclerosis and, 140-41
    cholesterol and, 140
    congestive heart failure and, 27
    heart disease and, 19-20, 73, 76, 78,
        84-86, 139-43, 161
    heart rate and, 140
    isometric, 141
    myocardial infarction and, 62, 76, 83-84
    sinus bradycardia and, 42
    smoking and, 141

F

Fainting. *See* Syncope

False-negative result, 168

False-positive result, 168

Fats. *See* Cholesterol, Diet

Fish oil
    heart disease and, 152
    triglycerides and, 152

Floppy valve syndrome, 36

Fluid retention. *See* Edema, pulmonary

Fluorocarbons
    arrhythmias and, 159
    heart disease and, 159

Fluoroscope, 36

Fluoroscopy, 16, 168

Framingham Heart Study
    cholesterol and, 144-45
    heart disease and, 21
    myocardial infarction and, 64, 144-45
    smoking and, 131-32

G

Gallstones, valve replacement surgery and, 40

Gemfibrozil, cholesterol reduction with, 149

Gender
    See also Women
    bypass surgery and, 91
    coronary artery disease and, 86
    myocardial infarction and, 64, 75-78

German measles (rubella), congenital heart
    defects and, 31

H

Hardening of the arteries. *See* Atherosclerosis

HDL. *See* Cholesterol, high density
    lipoprotein (HDL)

Health insurance, bypass surgery and, 98-99

Heart
    function of, 4-10
    location of, 3
    structure of, 3, 4, 7-10

Heart attack. *See* Myocardial infarction

Heart block, 42, 47, 169

Heart disease
    See also Angina pectoris, Arrhythmias,
        Cardiomyopathy, Congenital heart defects,
        Congestive heart failure, Ischemia,
        Myocardial infarction, Pericarditis,
        Valvular heart disease
    alcohol and, 143-44
    beta carotene and, 155
    children and, 160-62
    cholesterol and, 19, 86, 144-55, 161
    diet and, 144-55, 161
    exercise and, 84-86, 139-43
    fish oil and, 152
    Framingham Heart Study and, 21
    hormones and, 20, 21
    hypertension and, 136
    lecithin and, 152
    lithium and, 156
    mortality and, 156-57, 160
    niacin and, 154-55
    occupational hazards and, 159
    potassium and, 153-54
    pregnancy and, 162-63
    prevention of, 127-55
    Pritikin Diet and, 150-51
    race and, 20, 158
    risk factors for, 19-23, 128-39, 155, 161
    selenium and, 155
    smoking and, 19, 66, 73, 76, 78, 81, 86,
        96, 128-35, 152, 155, 161
    stress and, 137-39
    surgery, noncardiac and, 159
    travel and, 157-58
    triglycerides and, 150, 161
    vitamins and minerals and, 153-55
    women and, 134
    zinc and, 155

Heart muscle disease. *See* Cardiomyopathy

Heart rate, exercise and, 140

Heart transplant, 113-15

Heart valve disease. *See* Valvular heart disease

Heart, artificial, 111-12

Heartbeat, irregular. *See* Arrhythmia,
    Bradycardia, Tachycardia

Hemoglobin, 169

High blood pressure. *See* Hypertension

Histamine, cardiac deaths and, 21-22

Holiday heart syndrome, 144

Hormones
    cancer and, 77
    myocardial infarction and, 20-21, 76-77
    stress and, 137

Hospitalization
  congestive heart failure and, 27
  myocardial infarction and, 67, 82-83

Hydralazine, 28

Hydrocarbons, heart disease and, 159

Hypercholesterolemia, 145, 169

Hypertension, 169
  angiotensin converting enzyme (ACE)
    inhibitors and, 29-30
  arterioles and, 136, 166
  atherosclerosis and, 136
  beta blockers and, 83, 167
  children and, 161-62
  ethnic groups and, 158
  heart disease and, 19-20, 66, 73, 83, 86,
    102, 136, 167
  magnesium and, 153
  race and, 158
  smoking and, 129-30

Hyperthyroidism, 169, cholesterol and, 147

Hypertriglyceridemia, 150, 169

Hypertrophy, 169, congestive heart failure
  and, 25-26

Hypnosis, smoking and, 135

Hypotension, 169

Hypothermia, 169, sinus bradycardia and, 42

Hypothyroidism, 169, sinus bradycardia and, 42

Hypoxia, 169, arrhythmias and, 40

I

Indigestion
  angina and, 58
  myocardial infarction and, 63, 65

Infarction, 169, extension of, 72. *See also*
  Myocardial infarction

Infections, bypass surgery and, 94

Informational and mutual aid groups, 164

Insulin, heart disease and, 21

Invalidism
  bypass surgery and, 93-94
  myocardial infarction and, 67-68

Ischemia, 56-57, 169
  angioplasty and, 103
  arrhythmias and, 40
  magnesium and, 153
  stress and, 137

Ischemic heart disease. *See* Angina, Ischemia,
  Myocardial infarction

J

Jarvik 7, 112

K

Kidney failure, pericardial diseases and, 55-56

L

Lasers. *See* Angioplasty, laser coronary

LDL. *See* Cholesterol, low density
  lipoprotein (LDL)

Lead
  chelation therapy and, 116, 119
  heart disease and, 159

Lecithin, heart disease and, 152

Lidocaine, ventricular arrhythmias and, 43

Lipids. *See* Cholesterol

Lithium, heart disease and, 156

Liver pain, congestive heart failure and, 25

Lovastatin, cholesterol reduction with, 149

M

Magnesium
  digitalis toxicity and, 153
  sources of, 153

Magnetic resonance imaging (MRI), 170,
  murmurs and, 33

Malstress. *See* Stress

Mediastinum, 3, 170

Medicare
  diagnosis-related groups (DRGs) and, 51
  pacemaker fraud and, 48-50

Memory loss, bypass surgery and, 92-94

Menopause, myocardial infarction and, 76-77, 81

Mental impairment, bypass surgery and, 92-94

Minoxidil, 28, 55

Morphine sulfate, myocardial infarction
  and, 66-67

Mortality
  angioplasty and, 105
  bypass surgery and, 89-91
  diseases and, 160
  heart disease and, 87, 156-7, 160
  smoking and, 129-30

MRI. *See* Magnetic resonance imaging (MRI)

Murmurs, 23, 32, 36

Muscular dystrophy, cardiomyopathy and, 53

Myocardial infarction, 20, 170
  See also Infarction, 169
  angina and, 58, 63, 66, 101-2
  angioplasty and, 106
  arrhythmias and, 67
  aspirin and, 79-81
  beta carotene and, 155
  bilateral oophorectomy and, 81
  bypass surgery and future, 99, 101
  cardiac arrest and, 44, 72
  cardiopulmonary resuscitation (CPR) and, 66
  cause of, 62, 70, 85
  cholesterol and, 144-45
  congestive heart failure and, 70
  contraceptives, oral and, 81-82, 134
  coronary artery disease and, 86
  diagnosis of, 63, 65
  estrogen and, 76-77
  familial links to, 75
  fish oil and, 152
  Framingham Heart Study and, 64, 144-45
  indigestion and, 65
  invalidism and, 67-68
  magnesium and, 153
  menopause and, 76-77, 81
  niacin and, 154
  nitrates and, 159
  potassium and, 154
  prevention of, 73, 76-81
  rate decline, 77-78
  risk factors for, 64, 66, 73, 75-78, 81-82,
    85, 127-34
  self help and, 110, 140
  sexual relations and, 74
  sickle cell anemia and, 20
  silent attacks, 65-66
  smoking and, 128
  surgery, noncardiac and, 81, 159
  survival after, 73
  symptoms of, 63
  treatment for, 43-44, 66-71, 82-84
  vasectomy and, 79
  ventricular aneurysm and, 70, 173
  ventricular fibrillation and, 42-43, 72
  women and, 64, 75-77, 81-82, 134

Myocardium, 4, 34, 170

N

Necrotic tissue, 70, 170, myocardial infarction
  and, 62, 70

Niacin
  cholesterol and, 149
  heart disease and, 154-55
  side effects of, 154-55
  sources of, 154

Nicotinamide. *See* Niacin

Nicotine, 132

Nicotinic acid. *See* Niacin

Nifedipine, 28

Nitrates, heart disease and, 159

Nitroglycerin, 28, 58, 60-61, 63, 67, 102

Nitroprusside, 28

Nodes, 166, 172
  atrioventricular, 10, 166
  sick sinus node syndrome, 42, 47, 171
  sinoatrial, 9, 172

Noise pollution, heart disease and, 21, 159

O

Obesity, heart disease and, 19, 66, 73

Occlusion, 62, 170, myocardial infarction
  and, 62

Occupational hazards, heart disease and, 159

Omega-3 fatty acid fish oil, 152

P

Pacemakers
  arrhythmias and, 46-51
  complications with, 48
  costs associated with, 51
  evaluation standards for, 50
  function of, 46-47
  heart block and, 47
  Medicare fraud and, 48-50
  Nader, Ralph and, 49
  peer review committees and, 51
  second opinions with, 50
  sinus node problems and, 47

Patent ductus arteriosus, 34

Percutaneous transluminal coronary angioplasty
  (PTCA). *See* Angioplasty, percutaneous
  transluminal coronary (PTCA)

Pericardial effusion, 55-56, 171

Pericardiocentesis, 171, pericardial effusion
  and, 56

Pericarditis, 54-56, 165, 171
  acute nonspecific, 55, 165
  acute, 55, 165
  cardiac tamponade, 56, 167
  congenital defects and, 56
  constrictive, 56, 167
  pericardial effusion, 55-56, 171
  treatment for, 55-56
  tumors and, 56

Pericardium, 4, 54, 171

Peripheral mechanisms, congestive heart failure
  and, 26

The Pill. *See* Contraceptives, oral

Placebo, 171

Plaque, 57, 71, 86, 171
  angina and, 57
  atherosclerosis and, 171
  cholesterol and, 146
  coronary artery disease and, 86
  myocardial infarction and, 62, 70-71

Pleurisy, 58, 171

Pneumonia and influenza, 160

Potassium
  heart disease and, 153-54
  sources of, 154

Poverty, heart disease and, 19

Prazosin, 28

Pregnancy, heart disease and, 162-63

Pritikin Diet, 150-51

Procainamide, 44

Propranolol
  arrhythmias and, 43
  congestive heart failure and, 44
  digitalis toxicity and, 43
  myocardial infarction and, 43-44, 83-84

Q

QRS complex, 13

Quinidine, tachyarrhythmias and, 43

R

Race
  bypass surgery and, 99-100
  heart disease and, 20, 158
  hypertension and, 158

Radiation
  children and, 162
  pericardial disease and, 55-56

Resuscitation, physical external.
  See Cardiopulmonary resuscitation (CPR)

Retirement, heart disease and, 22

Rheumatic fever, 35-36, 171

Rheumatoid arthritis, angina and, 57

Roto-rooter therapy. *See* Coronary atherectomy

Running, sinus bradycardia and, 42

S

Sclerosis, 86, 171

Selenium
  cardiomyopathy and, 52
  heart disease and, 155

Self help, myocardial infarction and, 110-11

Sex differences, coronary artery disease
  management and, 64

Sexual relations
  bypass surgery and, 93-94
  myocardial infarction and, 74

Shock, myocardial infarction and, 62

Sick sinus node syndrome, 42, 47, 171

Sickle cell anemia, heart disease and, 20

"Silent heart attack", 65-66

Sinus nodes. *See* Nodes, sinoatrial

Smoking
  angina and, 131
  atherosclerosis and, 132-33
  cancer and, 130, 132-33
  cholesterol and, 129-30
  contraceptives, oral and, 134
  exercise and, 141
  Framingham Heart Study and, 131-32
  heart disease and, 19, 66, 73, 76, 78, 81,
    86, 96, 128-35, 152, 155, 161
  hypertension and, 129-30
  mortality and, 129-30
  myocardial infarction and, 128
  passive, 133-34
  quitting, 131, 135

Snuff, heart disease and, 133

Sodium, congestive heart failure and, 27

Sodium dextrothyroxine, cholesterol reduction
  with, 149

Sphygmomanometer, 11, 172

Stenosis
  angina and, 57
  angioplasty and re-, 105-6
  aortic, 24, 166
    congestive heart failure and, 24
  pulmonary valve, 33-34, 162
  valvular heart disease and, 36

Sternum, 4, 172

Stethoscope, 11, 36, 59, 172

Streptokinase, 172
  angioplasty and, 103
  myocardial infarction and, 68-69, 71

Stress
  angina and, 60
  arrhythmias and, 137
  behavior therapy and, 138-39
  coronary artery spasms and, 137
  heart disease and, 19, 22, 66, 73, 76,
    85-86, 137-39
  hormones and, 137
  ischemia and, 137
  type A personalities and, 137, 139

Stress test, 14, 59, 65-66, 85, 172

Stroke
  bypass surgery and, 93
  clot busting drugs and, 69

Suggested reading, 174-75

Support groups, 164

Surgery
  bilateral oophorectomy, 81, 167
  bypass, 39, 61, 94-108, 110-11, 116-7
  coronary artery disease and, 87
  cardiomyopathy and, 54
  congenital heart defects and, 31-34
  congestive heart failure and, 27
  heart disease and noncardiac, 159
  myocardial infarction and, 81
  open heart for children, 162
  pericardial diseases and, 55-56
  pulmonary valve stenosis in children and, 162
  valve replacement, 37-40, 159
  ventricular aneurysm and, 70

Syncope, 53, 172, cardiomyopathy and, 53

Systemic lupus erythematosus, angina and, 57

Systole, 10, 172

T

T.P.A. *See* Tissue-type plasminogen activator (T.P.A.)

Tachycardia, 26, 172
  atrial paroxysmal, 42, 166
  congestive heart failure and, 26

Tetralogy of Fallot, 33-34

Thromboembolism, 38-39, 127, 172

Thrombosis, 62, 68, 71, 172

Thrombus, 172

Tissue-type plasminogen activator (T.P.A.), 172,
  myocardial infarction and, 69

Tobacco, chewing, heart disease and, 133

Tranquilizers, sinus bradycardia and, 42

Transplant, heart, 113-15

Travel, heart disease and, 157-58

Treadmill. *See* Stress tests

Triglycerides, 173
  See also Cholesterol
  fish oil and, 152
  heart disease and, 150, 161
  hypertriglyceridemia, 150, 169
  women and, 150

Tuberculosis, 56, 160

Tumors, valvular heart disease and, 36

Type A personalities, stress and, 137, 139

U

Ultrasound, murmurs and, 33

V

Valve replacement surgery, 37-40
  antibiotics and, 39
  anticoagulants and, 39
  bypass and, 39
  complications with, 38-40
  surgery, noncardiac and, 159

Valves, 7-9
  aortic, 9, 166
  function of, 35
  mitral, 9, 170
  pulmonic, 9, 171
  replacement, 38
  tricuspid valve, 9, 173

Valvular heart disease
  angiography and, 36-37
  annuloplasty and, 37, 165

cardiac catheterization and, 36-37
  commissurotomy and, 37, 167
  coronary artery disease and, 39
  diagnosis of, 36-37
  endocarditis, 35-36, 168
  floppy valve syndrome, 36
  murmurs and, 36
  rheumatic fever and, 35-36, 171
  stenosis and, 36
  surgery and, 36-39
  tumors and, 36
  valvular regurgitation, 35, 173

Valvular regurgitation, 35, 173,
  cardiomyopathy and, 52

Vasectomy, myocardial infarction and, 79

Vasodilators, 173
  angina and, 60-61
  captopril, 28
  congestive heart failure and, 28
  hydralazine, 28
  insulin, 21, 173
  minoxidil, 28
  nifedipine, 28
  nitroglycerin, 28, 58, 60-61, 63, 67, 102
  nitroprusside, 28
  prazosin, 28

Veins, 173
  inferior vena cava, 5, 169
  superior vena cava, 5, 172

Ventricles, 4-5, 170, 173

Ventricular aneurysm, 70, 173,
  myocardial infarction and, 70

Ventricular assist device, 112-13

Ventricular fibrillation, 173,
  myocardial infarction and, 42-43, 72

Ventricular hypertrophy, 34, 171

Ventricular septal defect, 33-34

Ventricular tachycardia, magnesium and, 153

Vitamin A. *See* Beta carotene

Vitamin B-3. *See* Niacin

Vitamins and minerals, heart disease and, 153-55

W

Women
  bypass surgery and, 91
  heart disease and, 134
  myocardial infarction and, 64, 75-77, 134
  pregnancy and heart disease, 162-63
  triglycerides and, 150

X

X rays, murmurs and, 32

Z

Zinc, heart disease and, 155